"If you are ready to succeed on your own terms by being fully, unapologetically *you*, you will relish the pages of *Be*. Jessica not only gives you expert strategies to build your platform, she will boost your confidence, light a fire in your heart, and remind you why you are worthy of having it all. Come for the expert personal branding advice; stay for the spiritual inspiration and personal empowerment. Jessica's personal branding expertise is what every female entrepreneur needs to know."

REBECCA MINKOFF

"If I could bottle up the magic it takes to get from where you are to where you want to be, this book would be it. It's not a self-help book; it's a story about becoming *your* you. It'll strip away your ego and conspire with your inner voice to get you doing what you always knew you should. *Be* ready for change."

LADI GREENSTREET

head of European investments, Accenture Ventures

"Our power exists not in our doing, but in our *being*. Jessica takes us on an expert journey to discover our Truth, our real 'personal brand,' and gives us the permission to simply be who we were born to be."

SHAMAN DUREK

"If your goal is to have your dream business and life, Jessica is going to let you in on some of the biggest secrets to creating this for yourself. All the strategy and knowledge in the world is *not* what people are buying into—people want a relationship and buy into *the realest* version of you. The more real you show up, the more of a magnet for all your desires you become. This book teaches you what being 'real' means for you, how to accept and move past your mistakes quickly, and how to create powerful networks and die-hard audiences by being human AF."

LORI HARDER

bestselling author, *Forbes* top-rated podcast host, founder of Lite Pink

"*Be* is an incredible book to remind you to tap into your fullest expression and blossom into the butterfly that you are."

SAHARA ROSE

bestselling author and podcast host

"Jessica has a divine talent for distilling complex competencies into useful and purposeful plans. *Be* is no exception. It's chock-full of strategies for building a comprehensive and intentional personal brand that will take you so much further in life than you had ever planned. This book is a fantastic resource for anyone trying to get a grasp on who they are and how they show up in the world."

DANNIE LYNN FOUNTAIN

Google

"Jessica's blunt and bold approach to business is *Be*-yond inspiring. Letting go of the ledge and taking the leap to do what you love in life is a challenge made easier by reading this badass book."

ALISON VICTORIA

HGTV

"*Be* is a wonderful book to guide you on an enjoyable path to realizing your dreams while saving countless headaches along the way. I love Jessica Zweig's refreshing approach to business and life. She has reminded me to be myself and remember that is enough to reach my wildest dreams. If you want to help people and feel good in the process, *Be* is the book for you."

TARA STILES

Founder of Strala Yoga and best selling author

"Jessica has written a self-empowerment manifesto for emerging leaders. If you want to build your personal brand, this book is a must. And if you want to stay current and relevant through self-development and creating a framework for a bright future, this book will be transformational."

TONY HUNTER

CEO of McClatchy Company and Founder, TWH Enterprises.

Be.

A No-Bullsh*t Guide
to Increasing
Your Self-Worth and
Net Worth by Simply
Being *Yourself*

JESSICA ZWEIG

sounds true
WAKING UP THE WORLD

Be.

A No-Bullsh*t Guide
to Increasing
Your Self-Worth and
Net Worth by Simply
Being *Yourself*

JESSICA ZWEIG

Sounds True
Boulder, CO 80306

Published 2021, 2023

Cover design by Tara DeAngelis
Book design by Linsey Dodaro
Artwork by Aleksa Narbutaitis
Author photo © Lindsey Smith

Printed in the United States of America

BK06614

ISBN: 978-1-64963-050-6

The Library of Congress has cataloged the hardcover edition as follows:

Names: Zweig, Jessica, author.
Title: Be : a no-bullsh*t guide to increasing your self worth and net worth
   by simply being yourself / Jessica Zweig.
Description: Boulder : Sounds True, 2021.
Identifiers: LCCN 2020028200 (print) | LCCN 2020028201 (ebook) | ISBN
   9781683646990 (hardback) | ISBN 9781683647003 (ebook)
Subjects: LCSH: Branding (Marketing) | Social media. | Creative ability in
   business. | Success in business.
Classification: LCC HF5415.1255 .Z94 2021 (print) | LCC HF5415.1255
   (ebook) | DDC 650.1--dc23
LC record available at https://lccn.loc.gov/2020028200
LC ebook record available at https://lccn.loc.gov/2020028201

10 9 8 7 6 5 4 3 2 1

FSC
www.fsc.org
MIX
Paper | Supporting
responsible forest
FSC® C10309

Do not be surprised
how quickly the
Universe will respond
once you have <u>decided.</u>

To Mom and Dad, for every opportunity to **Be**.

To Rea, for the constant reminder to **Be**.

To Brian, for the wings to **Be**.

CONTENTS

Preface   ix

INTRODUCTION: How I Came to Be.   1

PART 1: **BE. REAL**

CHAPTER 1: Embrace Your Shit   11

CHAPTER 2: No One Cares   21

CHAPTER 3: The Generosity Economy   29

CHAPTER 4: So . . . What Is Personal Branding?   35

PART 2: **BE. YOUR BRAND**

CHAPTER 5: How to Play the (Long) Game   47

CHAPTER 6: Your Mess(age) Is Your Magic   59

CHAPTER 7: Introducing the Personal Brand Hologram   67

CHAPTER 8: Create Endless Content with the Supernova   83

CHAPTER 9: It's All Been Said Before   97

CHAPTER 10: Thought Leaders Think   109

CHAPTER 11: Introducing the Pinnacle Content Framework   115

CHAPTER 12: Shoot for the Stars   135

CHAPTER 13: Introducing Orion's Roadmap   141

CHAPTER 14: Pitch Like a Pro   151

CHAPTER 15: Get Your (Social Media) Mind Right   165

CHAPTER 16: The Ten Evergreen Principles of Social Media   175

PART 3: **BE. FREE**

CHAPTER 17: Everything Is Energy   191

CHAPTER 18: Color Your Life   201

CHAPTER 19: The Future of Business Is . . .   211

CHAPTER 20: Freedom Redefined   225

CHAPTER 21: Be Your Own Hero   229

CHAPTER 22: Find Your Edges   235

CHAPTER 23: Simply Be.   245

Afterword   249

Acknowledgments   251

Notes   255

About the Author   257

All worksheets available
for download at

jessicazweig.com/be

PREFACE

I was sitting in my home office in my apartment in Chicago, staring blankly at my bank balance.

My checking account was -$113.09. I had already borrowed money from my boyfriend. I had promised to pay him back, knowing the future of our relationship depended on it.

I was running my own business at the time, a popular online magazine for women. Between the six separate credit card accounts we had opened to help run the business, we were collectively over $75,000 in debt. Perhaps worst of all, my phone bill was overdue. And I *needed* my phone. Without it, I could not run my fledgling business, keep my audience engaged via social media, check my email for the unlikely news that I was closing a deal, and stay in contact with my then business partner, who I not so secretly resented for our situation. With no money in either my business or personal account and zero clients in the pipeline, I had no idea where I was going to find $250 to pay AT&T. I was desperate.

I got dressed, walked down to the parking lot of my building, started up my ancient Honda Accord, and drove forty-five minutes north to my parents' house in the suburbs. My mom and dad were sitting in the kitchen, drinking coffee, and rummaging through the Sunday paper. They looked delighted and grateful to see their busy, successful, entrepreneurial thirty-three-year-old daughter.

Their smiles faded as I explained to them, well, *everything*. My father is the one person I had worked my entire life to make proud, and I will never forget the look on his face. He was not angry. He wasn't even disappointed. To be either would have meant he understood what I was actually saying. He looked, quite honestly, confused. My mom, the quintessential Jewish mother, exuded sheer worry. I tried to make it clear I wasn't coming to them to bail me out. I just needed $250 to pay off my phone bill so I could still operate my business. Even though I was terrified about my future, I knew what a privilege it was to even have parents who could me help out with that kind of request. This made the humiliation even worse.

To be frank, the rest of our conversation that day remains a blur. What I *do* remember is walking out of my parents' house with a check in hand for $500, sobbing uncontrollably with shame.

In that moment, I made a vow to turn my life around. And I *could* sit here and tell you that I did. You *could* easily assume, simply by looking at the picture of my life as it stands today, that I finally figured it all out.

Yes, I currently run a seven-figure business, the SimplyBe. Agency, an internationally award-winning personal branding firm, servicing clients from Silicon Valley to New York, Europe, and Asia. Yes, I develop the personal brands of CEOs and entrepreneurs who have built multi-million and billion dollar companies. Yes, I get paid to travel the world, speaking on the topic of authenticity and teaching masterminds on the power of personal branding in places like Bali and Costa Rica. Yes, I have been featured as a "personal branding expert" on today's top media platforms, including *Forbes*, *Inc.*, MarketWatch, and HuffPost. And yes, that boyfriend eventually became my husband, and today I am the breadwinner of our family.

So things worked out, right? Yes and no. Because that's only part of the story.

Throughout the many rock-bottom moments I have experienced in the past decade of my career, whether that was going through a bloody professional divorce with that old business partner of mine, taking a corporate gig I loathed for financial security shortly thereafter, offering investors I barely knew over 60 percent of a new company because I believed I needed their money, demoting myself within another agency who wanted my brand name because I felt like I needed their validation after those investors backed out, or going broke at thirty-three and asking my parents to help me pay my phone bill while simultaneously running the most popular women's magazine in the city, it all came down to one thing:

My self-worth.

If I look back at every moment of success I have experienced in the past few years, each of them has been directly associated with a very simple belief: that I was enough, and the only way out is through.

There is a misconception about net worth, and it says that in order to have a lot of it, you have to go to a really great college. Or be born into it. Or have a great resume in order to achieve certain corporate positions. Or even be the type of person who just works really, really hard. I believe that's all bullshit.

People who live in abundance, financially speaking, all have one thing in common: They feel, at their core, that they deserve it. That they are worthy of it. Self-worth is the cause; net worth is the effect. All the high-paying retainers I've earned, the five-figure speaking fees I've charged, the press hits I've accrued, the talented team I've attracted, the millions of dollars in revenue I've grown, and even the relationships I've successfully maintained happened *after* I finally chose to believe that I was worthy of all of it.

Flaws, fears, mistakes, and failures included.

When you free yourself to simply be yourself, your confidence grows, your joy expands, and your value increases. This is a daily practice, not a destination. At least it's been mine. In picking up this book, you have officially begun your own journey toward simply being.

At its core, this is a book about being in your truth. It's about living that truth. And you must come to learn—just as I did—that you are worthy of *sharing* that truth. Once you do, your life and your career become unstoppable.

That's because your truth is your superpower, your magic, and your competitive advantage. It's what I like to call your personal brand—which is, quite simply, how you show up for the world. It's the platform you build around your truth that, when communicated consistently, constantly, and clearly, becomes an invaluable asset for achieving success beyond your wildest dreams.

There are so many misperceptions about what the term *personal brand* even means. In these pages I am going to bust the myths, redefine the concept altogether, and hold you accountable to building yours. The more you become willing to show up *authentically*, the more magnetic you become as a person and as a professional.

And what do magnets do?

They *attract*.

It's therefore no surprise that the most authentic people are always the most magnetic ones, and thus the individuals who seem to effortlessly attract their ideal opportunities, clients, and revenue. You can and *will* become one of those people too. Because you actually already are. I'm going to teach you step-by-step how to uncover it.

HOW I CAME TO BE.

"You can either stand inside your story
and <u>own it</u>, or stand outside your story
and hustle for your worthiness."

Brené Brown

I grew up an awkward, gawky girl with frizzy hair, terrible acne, and about twenty pounds of baby fat that stuck around until I was twenty-one. I was ruthlessly teased by the mean girls and bullied by the even meaner boys. In high school, I found a home in the theater department, surrounded myself with the other suburban misfits, and, quite literally, pretended to be someone I wasn't.

As if my insecurities weren't palpable enough, I went off to college to study theater and became a professional actress. After graduation, I lived the quintessential artist life, dabbling in cocktail waitressing, nannying, and temping, and all the while getting rejected on the regular at auditions and trying to stay—well—*not broke.*

In 2008, at the ripe age of twenty-six, I met a girl at one of those temp jobs, and we became fast friends. Three months later, fueled by our love of trying out new restaurants in Chicago, we decided to become business partners. After endless hours of researching what it took to actually run a business, let alone build one, we wrote a hundred-plus-page business plan defining what would become the largest online women's lifestyle magazine for seven years straight: CheekyChicago.com (Cheeky). We raised some money from friends and family, quit our temp jobs, and became cofounders. Each week, we published over thirty articles on the hippest restaurants, bars, and nightclubs, reported on the latest fashion and fitness trends, featured local celebrities and national lifestyle experts, and covered up-and-coming destinations in arts and culture. This was at the dawn of social media, and we were early adopters. As a result, Cheeky exploded. We quickly reached over one hundred thousand local readers and partnered with hundreds of brands as our clients. We also threw the sickest parties in town.

I became an "It Girl" in Chicago practically overnight, with my photo seen in every monthly glossy socialite magazine. I was regularly featured in TV segments on NBC, ABC, and FOX as a social media and lifestyle expert. My personal brand was starting to grow (albeit unconsciously), and it felt like the whole city knew who I was. You can only imagine how cool and self-important this made me feel, having never been considered a member of the popular crowd until that moment in my adulthood.

From the outside in, Cheeky looked like a super-hip start-up, led by two sparkly, social, stylish founders who preached women's empowerment.

What was happening on the inside was a very different story.

Our business partnership was toxic. We actually hated each other. I suffered from constant anxiety attacks and depression and eventually contracted an autoimmune disease from all the stress. I was going out six nights a week, and usually drinking too much, in the pursuit of "being seen." Back at the office, our advertising revenue model was too cyclical to sustain itself, and we could barely pay our employees, let alone ourselves.

I knew I needed a shift, but I could not figure out how to make one. The magazine, despite its dysfunctionality, was my life. It was my entire identity. It was *me*. How on earth could I stop doing it?

The day I found myself at my parents' house in the suburbs asking them to help me pay my phone bill was around the same time I started experiencing regular panic attacks and emotional breakdowns. There was one particular meltdown where I found myself looking down at my wrist, eyes welled with tears, and staring at the tiny tattoo written across it, which said, "Simply be." It had been there for years. It was in that moment that, for the first time in my life, I heard a *very* loud, *very* distinct, *completely undeniable* inner voice, my higher self. She said, "No matter what you do after Cheeky—and you *will* do something else—name your next company Simply Be. as a reminder to always be in alignment with your truth. Because right now, you're not. And something has to change."

I ended up leaving Cheeky soon after to do just that. (Once you hear the truth from your higher self, you can't unhear it.) And when I did, something remarkable happened. I made the announcement I was leaving to start my one-woman consultancy called—you guessed it—the SimplyBe. Agency with a launch strategy that consisted of two tactics. The first was an email I sent to my network bcc'ing a couple hundred people announcing my departure and that SimplyBe. was open for business. The second was a Facebook post.

Within one business week, I had over $20,000 worth of client retainer work and a line out the door. This was my aha moment on the power of a personal brand. At that juncture in my career, I didn't even realize I had one myself. What's more, I realized that no one who had hired me *actually* understood what I did. All they knew was the story I had been unconsciously telling about myself online for the previous seven years as the founder of a seemingly successful digital magazine. It was enough information for my prospective clients that I didn't have to make a single sales phone call to launch an entirely new business. I thought to myself, "Shit, if I did this *accidentally*, what could I do if I got *intentional*?"

I learned quite quickly that when done effectively, intentionally, and authentically, a strong personal brand can be the most powerful business asset you can possess. In fact, it could become the only marketing tool you will *ever* need. That's because people do business with *real people*, not logos, websites, mastheads, or Instagram channels.

However, before I could go forth and build a personal brand rooted in truth and authenticity, I had to get clear about my own truth first. And this didn't happen overnight. It took years of work, an expensive life coach, and most of all, a willingness to own my side of the mess I had created at Cheeky. To fully acknowledge that I was showing up without integrity and in total misalignment with my purpose. What's more, I realized how much I had been dimming my own light to make my business partner feel comfortable, and, in an effort to avoid conflict, how much I had lied to her as a result. I finally acknowledged that I had a horrible relationship with money and needed to become responsible enough to not spend money I did not have. I grew to understand that the world would only mirror back to me the money I felt I was worthy of making, and *that* was the real reason I was broke. I had to finally own that I was living a lie. That it was all bullshit.

As I moved forward to launch the SimplyBe. Agency, I made the decision to do things very, very differently this time around. I knew this time, my entrepreneurial business was going to be a direct expression of my values, my strengths, and my truth. I was going to surround myself with only the highest vibrational people. I was going to shelve my ego and focus on helping other people, but I was also going to charge more money for my value and time. Finally, and perhaps the most powerful choice of all, I decided to share my story with anyone who would listen. The real story—unapologetically, unabashedly, and authentically. The good, the bad, the ugly, the shameful, the glamorous, the piss poor. Online. Offline. With old friends and new colleagues on panels, on my blog, on social media, and in my newsletter. I decided to use my authentic personal brand platform in the service of my business and my mission.

It was at this precise inflection point that everything shifted. I started to attract *incredible* clients and top talent to my company, I got paid to speak to share my story, I hit national PR outlets, and I began making more money than I ever had in my life.

I am not saying it was smooth sailing, because it never is. I am sharing this to demonstrate that as soon as you get into alignment with your truth and lead with a personal brand that is full of humanity, service, intention, and *your story*—the game changes. As soon as you uplevel your self-worth, your net worth responds in kind.

This is the sauce.

As soon as I figured out how to simply be me, everything expanded. The instant I decided I was worthy of sharing myself, my stories, my realness (financially and personally) with my clients, my team, the media, and my social media followers, my business took off. I now live and breathe unapologetic authenticity with every decision I make. This is the Kool-Aid I serve daily to my clients and sip myself.

While this is a book about personal branding, this is not your typical personal branding book. To be frank, I find most books on personal branding to be full of shit. Sure, they might teach you how to curate a perfect Instagram feed, create the magic bullet to make your blog go viral, or get yourself on the stages of TED without ever asking the question, "WHO AM I?" in the first place, and perhaps more importantly, "WHY SHOULD PEOPLE CARE?"

Sorry, I didn't mean to yell. I'm just fired up about the notion of people fully waking up to the power of their true, authentic *message*—their *real* personal brand. I get miffed watching so many personal branding "experts" talk pure tactics, pointing people to more followers and larger readership metrics in an effort to become "known." And hey, it's okay if you want to become known. Just ask yourself, "Known in service of what?"

I'm not diminishing the importance of what views, followers, subscribers, and fans can and will do for your platform. I am, however, stating that most people skip the most essential piece of what builds and sustains a personal brand platform over time:

Your *unapologetic authenticity*.

Your unapologetic authenticity is what will get people to come to your business, platform, or space, what will make them stay, and what will make them tell their friends and colleagues about you. The more authentic, real, and vulnerable you are, the more viral you actually become.

Authenticity is not rocket science. All it takes is a dose of courage, a dash of strategy, a shit ton of self-awareness, and a willingness to serve.

You see, it starts from within. It starts with really digging down inside the tiniest nooks and crannies, into the deepest depths of your desires, triumphs, failures, dreams, wounds, and one-of-a-kind life stories to reveal your *authentic personal brand*. Only then will you be able to architect a personal brand message that is real, meaningful, consistent, inspiring, original, and useful.

This book will teach you how to do exactly that.

In part 1, "Be. Real," you're going to learn once and for all the true meaning of "authenticity" and why you're worthy of sharing yours with the world. Expect to unlearn everything you've ever been told about personal branding. You'll find worksheets, assignments, and soul prompts that will remind you of your worthiness and inspire you to live your truth, and above all, *share* your truth with the world.

In the second part, "Be. Your Brand," you'll learn how to take this newfound understanding of branding yourself and use it to crystalize your authentic message and build an expert-level strategy to attract your ideal opportunities, clients, and customers to increase your net worth. I am opening up the freakin' vault to SimplyBe.'s best-in-class, trademarked methodologies, tools, templates, and frameworks. This is our process in building world-renowned personal brands, and I'm giving you access to it all.

We'll end our time together with part 3, "Be. Free." This is where your journey actually *begins*. You will learn how to take your authentic personal brand where it matters most: offline and into your relationships, human interactions, and work environments, so that you can become the *living* example of authenticity.

Finally, I'm going to encourage you to put the book down once and for all and go live your life. Because life is your teacher, and the further you reach into the depths of your soul and explore the edges of what's possible, the more inspired, real, brave, authentic, and impactful your message becomes.

Above all, you'll learn how to make your personal brand stand the test of time, because hey, life is long and Instagram might not be relevant ten years from now.

But this book will Be. And you can Be. too.

So, welcome to *Be.*, a guide to building *your* unapologetically authentic personal brand, with the precise actions and strategies that will take you from unknown expert to recognized thought leader, using the best marketing strategies, social media tactics, and PR hacks available.

But it will be your authentic true story that will be the ultimate guiding light, with me at the helm to help steer you each step of the way. Warning: This won't be a journey of rainbows and butterflies. That's not life, and that's certainly not business. This book will require an ample amount of self-discovery, self-awareness, and humility, an investment of your time, and a bit of ass-kicking. To be clear: this isn't just a guide; it's a *no bullshit* guide.

So buckle up, and get ready to Be. Your self-worth—and your net worth—are about to explode.

What a time to
be aligned.

PART 1: BE. REAL

CHAPTER 1

EMBRACE YOUR SHIT

"Wherever you go,
there you are."

Jon Kabat-Zinn

I learned the power of embracing my own shit over a decade ago.

I was going through one of the most difficult periods of my life: the end of a five-year relationship with a man fourteen years older than me. I was in my mid-twenties and up until then, I had never experienced that level of heartbreak. Breaking up with him felt like cutting off my own arm. My entire life was defined by that relationship, so when it ended, I was a shell of my former self.

I was also running Cheeky at this time. On the home page of the company website, there was a tiny section on the bottom right titled *Jessica's Blog*. (This was in 2009 when blogging was still a novelty.) I began to blog about my newly single life, and all that I was learning about myself. Week after week, I would take fingers to keyboard and let the truth of my experience with this heartbreak just pour out. Sure it was cathartic, but I also hoped that since my audience was mainly women, at least a *few* of them would undoubtedly relate. It turned out I was wrong.

There were thousands!

My blogs went viral. Each month, when I checked our Google Analytics, my personal blogs received at least 100 percent more engagement than our posts on the hottest new restaurants, workout fad, or Chicago celebrity sighting. I would get stopped on the street by women who had read my blogs, and they would relay to me how they shared them with all their friends across the country. This was my epiphany on sharing yourself authentically online.

The secret sauce to going viral is *vulnerability*.

This theory of mine didn't start and end with my breakup blogs back in 2009. I have seen it time and time again, all across the internet, for years. People have touched the masses, reached the media, and launched careers with this approach.

Vulnerability shouldn't be a one-trick pony. It should be the bedrock of your message. Whether it's a breakup, a divorce, a death, or just the lessons of daily life, the more vulnerability you share, the more infectious you become. Shit's powerful, and here's why:

Everyone has shit.

The more willing you are to reveal your shit, the more opportunity you have to create true brand affinity. People will listen to you because they can see themselves in you. Despite how big a company you have, how many people follow you on social media, or how many books you've sold, when you're real, you become accessible. People will resonate with your content, because you are, in fact, just like them.

Start by believing your shit is worth sharing and watch how you scale.

WHAT IS SHIT?

It's time to face your own shit. It's been waiting for you. There's nothing to be afraid of. Your shit is your friend, your edge, your magic. It's time for you to finally embrace it, and by that I mean to look your shit squarely in the face, claim it, own it, squeeze it, and give it a big THANK YOU. It's your biggest gift. It's time to wear your shit on your sleeve. (Not that kind of shit. Gross.)

Your shit doesn't mean your drama or your dirty laundry. It means your *realness*. It is the collection of all the things you have experienced in your life, professionally and personally, that have pierced your heart, broken you, lifted you up, shifted you, shaped you, and transformed you into who you are today. That's the shit I am talking about. And it's gold.

If the thought of putting all of your shit out into the world makes your stomach jump, riddle me this: Why do you think it feels so easy, fulfilling, and rewarding to spend your time with your closest friends? Because it's effortless. Why is it effortless? Because you don't have to hide your shit.

My best friend doesn't care that I talk to my dog more than I talk to her. My mom still loves me when I'm being a bitch. My girlfriends wear crystals in their bras too. (Rose quartz is great for enhancing the energy of love, citrine is the best for attracting abundance, and obsidian is the best for blocking out bad vibes, FYI.)

When you're among people who know the "real" you, there is no armor, no pretense, no "trying" to be. You get to just simply be. The same goes for when you're with yourself. Imagine if we were free to be ourselves all the time, despite occasion or company. Imagine a society where there were no proverbial masks. Imagine work environments where people felt as free to share their vulnerabilities as they did their triumphs. Imagine a world where people didn't hide what was *really* going on inside their heads or their hearts. Imagine a world where people embraced their shit.

Not only would we feel a heck of a lot lighter, but we would feel infinitely more fulfilled, connected, and *seen*. And this experience of full expression would not only benefit you as a person but the world as well. Seriously. Imagine if everyone was free to be vulnerable, free to be human. Not only would you as an individual feel better but everyone around you would cultivate deeper relationships and a deeper understanding of one another. And from where does all conflict arise? From not understanding the person next to us.

What's the first step toward embracing your shit? Your willingness to do so. Let's take some baby steps.

Consider the notion of small talk. Does it drain you? It sure does me. I would rather you tell me about your divorce or talk to me about racial justice than chitchat about the fucking weather. Think about it: Have you ever walked away from small talk and felt like you did anything other than waste time? Small talk is useless. Stop it now.

I know that sounds extreme, but when you're willing to get real, a couple of things happen. Your shit becomes less scary, because you'll soon discover that people have the same exact shit as you, and when you speak your truth to go beneath the surface, you instantly cut through the insecurities that exist in business and in life, and as a result, make real connections. Real connections are the foundation of any powerful business, brand, or platform.

Successful businesses start with people. And people are messy, complex, and beautiful. Therefore, an authentic business leader embraces his or her shit rather than hiding it.

Everyone, despite the money in our bank accounts, the city we live in, the clothes we wear, the homes we inhabit, the mistakes we make, and the families we were born into, is the same. We are intrinsically, fundamentally connected because we are all human.

A LOOK AT SHIT ACTUALLY EMBRACED

I want to make it clear that embracing your shit is not simply a tactic. You shouldn't use this approach to manipulate your audience. Using your authenticity as purely a strategy for more exposure is unfortunately why "authenticity" gets a bad rap in the first place.

Embracing your shit is about walking your talk. It's about ascribing your mess not only to a message but to a mission. It's about putting your money where your mouth is. The aim here should not be to go viral for vanity but for the purposes of impact. This requires a complete reframing of how you show up, not just online, but in every interaction you have and in every expression of your brand. This is where true authenticity is born: in the integration of your online and offline presence. At the intersection of what you are *doing* and who you are *being*.

This is another misconception. There is no distinction between your "professional brand" and your "personal brand." They are one and the same. Sure, you wear multiple hats, but this makes you a multidimensional individual, not a split personality. You aren't any different from 9:00 a.m. to 5:00 p.m. than you are from 5:00 p.m. to 9:00 a.m. Your beliefs, passion, personality, and *shit* should be infused into your entire personal brand.

Let's look at some of the most effective leaders, CEOs, and personal brands of our time. These are people who were not afraid to share their past, their humanity, their vulnerability, and their truth in the service of their companies, their audiences, and their missions. These are the people who are really embracing their shit.

Consider Gary Vaynerchuk, Oprah Winfrey, and Howard Schultz. What do they all have in common? Okay yes, they're all multimillionaires/billionaires, but that's not the point. Each and every one of them has led their businesses with their humanity. Their truth. Their war wounds. Their shit.

The founder of VaynerMedia, Gary Vaynerchuk, immigrated to this country when he was three years old, and his family had not a dollar to its name.[1] Oprah Winfrey suffered from sexual abuse. Starbucks CEO Howard Schultz grew up on welfare in the projects of Brooklyn and watched his family financially struggle due to his father's illnesses and their subsequent inability to pay his medical bills.

GaryVee has dedicated his career to helping aspiring entrepreneurs succeed. Oprah Winfrey taped over 200 *Oprah Winfrey Show* episodes that dealt with sexual abuse, more than any other topic. And as part of an unprecedented corporate policy, Howard Schultz made the choice to provide every part-time Starbucks employee with health insurance.

What's more, each one of these leaders has very publicly *shared* their personal stories of pain, resilience, and tenacity in order to bring a heightened level of purpose, relatability, and humanity to their brands. The distinction, however, is that they didn't exploit it. What they did instead was ascribe these personal setbacks to their brands' missions. As a result, they are now viewed as some of the greatest thought leaders of our time. Not because they are perfect, but because they are *real*.

That's the power of building a personal brand in service of your company. People don't do business with a logo; they do business with other people. And the sooner you lead from your humanity, the bigger your chances for impact.

YOUR SHIT DOESN'T STINK

Say you're the CEO of your company. Congratufuckinglations! While you may be the CEO, you're actually no different from your janitor. At the end of each day, you still take your pants off one leg at a time. So does he. You worry about the well-being of your kids. As does he. You're no better, and you're no worse. Sure, you have different credentials, experiences, skills, and incomes. But fundamentally, you're the same. You are both two people with fears, hopes, dreams, anxieties, moments of grandeur, and moments of failure. You are *human*. A great leader with a powerful personal brand understands this. When you see your janitor sweeping floors at the end of the day on your way out of the office, do you stop to say hello? Do you make him feel important? Can you see yourself in him?

Why does this matter? Because it's easy to become revered for your shit. You will quickly find that people, whether they're part of your organization, the media, or your social following, will become enamored of your raw authenticity and courageous vulnerability. This is wonderful, and an excellent net effect of your messaging. But adoration is not the end goal. Don't be too quick to trade the value of your struggle for the validation of your notoriety. I have seen this happen one too many times, and it's not a good look.

Case in point . . . me.

For most of my middle school and high school years, I was a legitimate nerd. So, ending up the founder of a successful lifestyle magazine later in life, I donned the moniker of "It Girl" proudly. As my social media following grew, so did my ego. For a long time, I felt like a mini celebrity. I truly believed that because people knew my name, and I could get into any night club I wanted, I was special. Perhaps, even a bit more special than most people.

But as soon as I walked away from Cheeky, the invites stopped coming. The free stuff in the mail stopped showing up. The features in the press dried up. No one seemed to care where I was, what I was doing, or who I was dating. After seven years of feeling like I was on top of the world, this was a hollow reckoning. I questioned my worth and my relevance. I had built my own personal brand at first by total accident, and in true earnestness for the women reading my blog going through similar circumstances. It took me quite some time to unpack that I had, rather unconsciously, grown my personal brand in service to myself.

I came to the realization that I had to chuck my ego and get back to the basics. I had once described my mess (my heartbreak) on Cheeky with my blog (my message) to help other women feel less alone and to create community (my mission). Somehow, I had forgotten that along the way. So with SimplyBe., I made the commitment to never lose sight of being in service again.

As you go forth and build your brand within the pages of this book and beyond, it's my belief that if you follow my strategies, formulas, and focus on authenticity, truth, and vulnerability, you will start to attract more people, opportunities, and attention to your brand. That's the goal. But don't come away from this thinking your shit makes you special. It doesn't. Remember you are sharing your humanity not for your sake, but for the sake of everyone around you. There is a critical distinction in personal brands who stay connected to their community and remember their roots, and the ones who don't.

MAKE YOUR SHIT SHINE

At this point you might be thinking one or all of the following:

- *"But I'm the face of my company."*
- *"I'm trying to be a good role model."*
- *"I am about to launch my next venture."*
- *"I'm about to graduate and start my career."*
- *"I have an image to uphold."*
- *"She can't be referring to me with all this shit about shit!"*

Actually, I am referring *specifically* to you.

Your shit is your edge. You see, brands don't have shit. Only people do. This is good news for you: there is a higher demand for authenticity online than ever before. Brands who are willing to subscribe to a mission resonate 80 percent better than those who don't.[2] But brands have been trying to do this for a long time. They spend millions and millions of dollars on an ad campaign to convey emotion, to display a personality, to strike a meaningful connection with their consumer. We, as people, inherently have the ability to architect a message both online *and* off that is rooted in emotion, personality, and connection. That's because we are human. No million dollar campaigns necessary.

If you want to be an effective leader, you need to be an infectious person. That starts with embracing your own humanity, your own heart, and your own authenticity. This is the first step on the path toward truly "Be.ing." To let your guard down and open up to your imperfections.

By now, you understand the true meaning of shit. It's time to uncover yours. Use the worksheet on the next page to unpack your biggest mess and to discover your message.

Every single person goes through a spectrum of emotions. No one has had it easy. Everyone has a battle scar, a skeleton in their closet, or a weakness they're not proud of. This is worth sharing, because it builds bridges and breaks down the barriers that separate us. Status is a fallacy. The sooner you realize that, the larger your chances are for positive impact. And positive impact, my friend, is the whole damn point.

UNCOVER YOUR SHIT

YOUR MESS

What has been your biggest personal challenge?

What has been your biggest professional challenge?

YOUR MESSAGE

How have you overcome it?

What was the greatest lesson you learned?

YOUR MISSION

Zero in on the moral of that story and ask yourself how it could inspire someone else in similar circumstances.

Be.
human

People don't do business with logos. We do
business with people. And the sooner you
lead from your humanity, the more
magnetic you become.

CHAPTER 2

NO ONE CARES

"Think lightly about yourself
and deeply about the <u>world</u>."

The biggest secret to personal branding is this: NO ONE CARES ABOUT YOU.

Guess what people care about?

Themselves.

All people are inherently self-involved. This doesn't make us bad people, it just makes us human.

Let me tell you a quick story. A few years back, a potential client came to my agency on a mission to be, in her words, the next Suze Orman. She was an extremely successful financial advisor who had decades of experience and expertise. She was in the process of launching a book along with an online course and wanted my agency's help in building her platform, which was nonexistent at the time. It was going to be a lot of work, and she was about to become my largest and most lucrative client.

During our first meeting, I asked her about her goals and vision for her brand and what she was looking to achieve. In the course of one hour, she talked exclusively about how she wanted a million subscribers on YouTube in less than one year, hundreds of thousands of email subscribers in six months, and enough Facebook fans to be a household name like Oprah.

At no point did she address how she wanted to *help* her clients. There wasn't a word about assisting them with saving for retirement, for example, or debt reduction for college students or navigating the merging of money for newly married couples or empowering women to become more financially independent or teaching empty nesters how to make the most of their savings. Her goals, objectives, milestones, and vision for her brand were all centered around *her*.

She was the first client I ever rejected.

If you come from a place of vanity, ego stroking, and a desire to be "famous," your clients will run for the hills faster than you can double tap your own Instagram photo. If your brand is all about *you*, then your brand is bullshit. And no one can smell bullshit quicker than your potential customers. This isn't a threat, just a reality.

If you're looking to become a YouTube star or Instafamous, I'm not your girl and this is not your book. I'm not saying that the net effect of the work we do together here won't help you achieve a large following and name recognition—in fact, it most definitely will—*but it is not the place we will start.*

You start by ascribing your personal brand to a mission, a vision, a philosophy, an ethos of something bigger than your own ego. This doesn't have to be lofty and grandiose. It just needs to have the simple, core objective of *helping other people* in some way. Create a personal brand that makes people *feel* something—seen, understood, empowered, inspired, valued, motivated, educated, connected—and watch how your clients, customers, and online followers begin to manifest not only in larger numbers but in a more meaningful capacity.

This isn't just feel-good reasoning. It's good business. In a recent report titled "Leveraging the Value of Emotional Connection for Retailers" by Motista, consumers with an emotional connection to a brand have a 306 percent higher lifetime value, stay with a brand for an average of 5.1 years versus 3.4 years, and will recommend brands at a much higher rate—71 percent versus 45 percent.[1] This is especially exciting for personal brands because brands aren't people. No one can connect to consumers the way people can; thus personal brands have the edge today, if you're willing to put in the work.

If that's not enough to motivate you to put meaning behind your messaging, consider the sheer volume of businesses and brands vying for attention. Social media is no longer social media, but simply, the internet. There are *billions* of people online today. The explosion of technology and innovation, with over one hundred million start-ups launched each year (that's three new companies per second), will ultimately drive even more competition in the marketplace for brands and people to get seen and heard.

We are living at an inflection point. For any brand, business, or individual, the game is no longer about eyeballs, but engagement. No longer about impressions, but impact. Content is no longer king, *clarity* is. Your best solution? Authenticity. Your best strategy? Service and generosity.

Reframe the narrative from "What can you do for me?" to "What am I here to give?" and watch how your message, your business, and your life expand.

BUT, REALLY, NO ONE CARES

As you start to build your brand, it's essential to first understand that when people come to the internet, social media platforms, the office, a panel, or a workshop or retreat, they're coming to better *their own lives*—their own careers, their own relationships, their own bodies, their own homes, their own families, their own mental well-being, and so on. They are *not* coming because they care about your relationships, how rich you might be, or how you're feeling today. This is the biggest misconception of them all.

If you're doing it right, personal branding is not an act of vanity but an act of service. It's not about what you can get (likes, accolades, attention, followers, and invites to cool parties) but about what you can give—your wisdom gleaned from life experiences and inspiration gleaned from triumphs or, more importantly, failures—in order to transform and impact the lives of others. It's about downplaying your ego and stepping forward with your authentic story to build a platform that will ultimately *serve* your clients, your consumers, your company, your culture, your teams, your community, and your digital audience.

This doesn't mean you should position yourself as a saint or a martyr. You, my friend, are human too. Just like your audience. Your mindset needs to be one of service. Your message has to be real.

Let's break this down.

Who you are *Be.ing*—with all your glorious flaws, endearing quirks, relatable failures, unique style, energy, and one-of-a-kind perspective—is your super-fucking-power. The more you show your humanity, the more magnetic you become.

That's because people do business with *people*. Ideally, people they like, trust, and most of all feel understood by. People don't want to do business with assholes.

When I tell people I run a personal branding firm, I can't tell you how often I get the response, "Wow, I bet your clients must have a lot of ego to invest in themselves that way." Or, my favorite, "So you, like, make people famous on the internet?"

With the rise of the social-media influencer and the reality-TV star, it's easy to think that investing time, energy, and money into your personal brand is seen as self-important and self-promotional.

Well, it is. But not in the way you think.

It comes down to worthiness. *Believe* that what you are here to do is worth doing, what you are here to say is worth saying, and what you are here to give is worth giving. This is the first step toward building an authentic, value-based message.

The second step is *self-promotion*. In order to spread your message far and wide to the people and communities that you are seeking to serve, you *must* self-promote. Otherwise, how on earth can you help the people who need your help and grow a business with sustainable impact? This isn't a reflection of your ego; it's a requirement for success. It's a pathway to net worth.

It takes totally reimagining not only the space of personal branding at large but your worthiness to create your own. The knee-jerk reaction people have to this work is generally judgment masked with an enormous layer of imposter syndrome.

It goes like this: "Ew, I don't want to be like *those* self-important people who do that *self-promotional thing*." (Judgment)

Once we get beyond the judgment, release the stigma, and consider the notion of doing this work ourselves, the thought is: "Who am I to promote myself? Why would anyone care what I have to say?" (Imposter syndrome)

My question is, "Who are you *not* to share your message?" No one else has your unique upbringing, education, career track, relationships, mistakes, triumphs, failures, lessons, learnings, or perspectives, which inherently provide you with something that no one else on the planet has: your value. It's a guarantee that there is someone out there (and more than likely *many* someones) who needs your message and doesn't even know it yet. That's because you don't even know it yet.

Building a personal brand message rooted *in service* to others is the antidote to unworthiness. It is judgment's neutralizer. It is imposter syndrome's cure.

By now, you hopefully understand not only your opportunity but your *responsibility* to share your brand. If you are in a unique position of leadership or expertise, or are embarking on the path toward it, then you are uniquely positioned to elevate your business in a way that no traditional marketing campaign ever can. We, the people, are the new media channels. And it's time we use these channels for good.

MAKE THEM CARE

One of my favorite clients of all time is Tony Hunter, the former CEO of the *Chicago Tribune*. Tony held several C-level positions from 2008 through 2016 and was part of the executive team that led the company out of bankruptcy. I'd heard wonderful things about Tony, and I was thrilled to get him into my agency. I'll never forget our first meeting when he came to our office and met my team.

After he introduced himself and gave a high-level overview of his objectives for engaging us—to help him write his book and launch his advisory services and speaking career—a rather outspoken, overly confident team member interjected and asked, "Excuse me for my naïveté here Tony, but there a lot of guys out there who look like you, who sound like you, and who want to talk about the same things you want to talk about. What is so special about you?"

Tony looked blankly at my team member, unresponsive.

Meanwhile, my heart was about to explode.

My team member went on: "There are a *million* C-suite guys out there who consider themselves 'experts' and want to get paid top dollar to speak. Why would I come to see you over the other guys? Why you? Why should someone care?"

Thank God Tony has a healthy ego. In fact, I believe he appreciated the challenge. He responded by saying, "No one's coming to see me. They're coming to see themselves. It doesn't matter that I was CEO. It doesn't matter that I successfully led a billion-dollar company and have the results to prove it. What matters is the people in the audience can see themselves in my story. I know many of them in the audience are walking through the fire, just like I did. I'm not standing on those stages for me. I'm standing on those stages to show emerging leaders that the fire doesn't kill you. If just one person in the audience walks away from my talk understanding that, and that alone, I've done my job."

As he began his personal branding journey, he recognized from the get-go that no one cared what he *did*. People cared about who he *was*. And therein lies all the difference. Be like Tony. I'll tell you how.

Use the worksheet to the right as a soul warm-up, a way of exploring your potential legacy and connecting with what you ultimately want to be remembered for. (Can I safely assume it's more than making

MAKE THEM CARE

What do you want people to say about you when you're not in the room?

I low do you want people to feel when you are?

What legacy do you want to leave?

a ton of money or seeing your name in lights?) Keep these answers close to you, as they will serve as the foundation for the service-based, mission-driven platform you're about to build in the coming chapters. Remember: when you make people feel, you make them care.

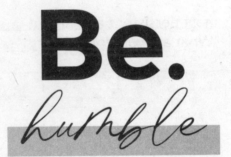

Be.
humble

The biggest secret about personal branding is this: no one cares. Building your brand is an act of service, not an act of ego. Remember that people inherently care about themselves, and that's ok. Be the type of brand (and person) who reminds your audience, clients and customers of their own power and potential.

CHAPTER 3

THE GENEROSITY ECONOMY

"Life's most persistent and urgent question
is 'What are you doing for <u>others</u>?'"

Dr. Martin Luther King Jr.

Your brain and heart are your two biggest assets. They are the most valuable assets you will ever earn or own.

From these assets are born wisdom and perspective. Whether it's a conversation over a coffee date, a blog post, an Instagram caption, or a keynote speech, these are your channels to share your value. Every time you approach your online platform, make new professional connections, or stand on a stage in front of an audience, no matter how big or small, ask yourself, "What is some of the best stuff I can give away here for free?"

Welcome to the Generosity Economy—a.k.a., personal branding done well. When you dedicate your personal brand to creating content, connection, and opportunities to share your value, you begin to build the foundation of your name, your platform, and your reputation. Give enough of your best stuff away for free, and you will slowly but steadily build an audience, a community, a client base that not only feels like they know, like, and trust you but subconsciously feels indebted to you. After all, you've given them so much without asking for something in return.

Ditch the scarcity mindset. This is tough for a lot of people. We hold our "best stuff" behind a proverbial fourth wall, making our clients, customers, and followers earn it. But the pathway from brand ambivalence to brand evangelism is paved in pure generosity. Know that there is enough to go around. Trust that if someone rips you off, that's their karma. Believe in the boomerang effect—the more quality content, clear communication, and good deeds you put out into the world, the more will come back to you.

ILLUMINATE. CAPTIVATE. MOTIVATE.

There's a popular marketing concept that promotes the idea that all content should "educate, entertain, or inspire," and that if you include one or more of these elements, you are doing it right and staying "in service" to your audience.

That's fine and well, and it checks a box. But it's probably not going to get you very far. This approach is tired, tactical, and two-dimensional. Great content *moves* people. It illuminates new ways of thinking, doing, and being. It captivates people with humor, audacity, and potential controversy. It motivates people to change their habits, their relationships, and their lives.

You can only do this when you deliver your message with unapologetic authenticity, fearless vulnerability, and deep generosity. Infuse your passion, your stories, and your unequivocal beliefs into your content. Set the intention to touch people's hearts and open people's minds. This is the foundation of any truly successful platform.

Let's do a real-time experiment. Go look up a thought leader, influencer, celebrity, or well-known executive you admire. Check out their website, podcast, or latest Instagram or Facebook post. Then ask yourself the following questions:

- *What is it exactly about the quality of their message that I love?*
- *What does it make me* feel?
- *Where do I feel it? In my heart, my stomach, my toes?*

- *Does it spark a new way of looking at my life, my job, the world?*
- *Does it motivate me to act, to change, to shift?*
- *Do I feel this person is talking directly to me, versus at me?*

If you're not checking these boxes with your own message, you're wasting time and creating nothing but noise. Let's do another experiment. Go look up an online thought leader, influencer, celebrity, or well-known expert who rubs you the wrong way. Study their latest content and posts. What exactly about them triggers you? Perhaps it's their messaging, tone, and aesthetic. But I'll bet that if you drill down deeper, it's actually quite simple: their content doesn't add any *value* for you.

Speaking of value, let's look at some of my favorite examples. Self-made people are my favorite kind of people, which is why I love Ramit Sethi, *New York Times* bestselling author and founder of iwillteachyoutoberich.com. Ramit came from a working-class family, put himself through Stanford, and has built an eight-figure business. But what I love most about him is that he's dedicated his career to teaching *others* how to become self-made too. He's built his business on the merit of his audience of millions, and he's grown that very audience by *illuminating* them through hundreds of free posts, each composed of tactical plans, scripts, how-tos, case studies, and guides on—you guessed it—how to become rich.

I'm obsessed with Josh Ostrovsky, more famously known as the "Fat Jewish." He started his Instagram account, @thefatjewish, in 2009, and his crude, gutsy, in-your-face and, at times, offensive humor was downright *captivating*. I find myself (almost literally) peeing my pants in laughter with a single Instagram post. Love him or hate him, it's hard to ignore him. It's also hard to ignore his eleven-plus million followers, his net worth of $80 million, and his inclusion on *Time* magazine's list of 30 Most Influential People on the internet.

I am also an enormous fan of author, speaker, and entrepreneur Danielle LaPorte. It's fair to say that her work has changed my life. Not because her platform is aesthetically beautiful and strategically executed (which it is) but because her personal stories of vulnerability and resilience have *motivated* me to look at my life from an entirely new perspective. Because of her work, my goals are not based on striving for achievement but simply on how I want to feel.

You don't need to have a success story like Ramit's, a comedic gift like Fat Jewish's, or a few bestselling books like Danielle's. You just have to know what you are really good at giving, and then go out and give it. Screw educating, entertaining, and inspiring people. Strive to illuminate, captivate, and motivate them instead.

WHAT ARE YOU HERE TO GIVE?

It can be hard to pinpoint exactly what our unique value proposition is. It's the thing you do that no one else can do in the way you do it. It's the essence of what you give when you're not even trying. It's the innate value you have when you are simply being. I'll be the first to admit that it's hard to put yourself into words. Sometimes we need a friend (or five) to help us out.

Pick three to five people in your life who know you the best. They should be a mix of professional and personal relationships. Think: your spouse, your boss, your mentor, your closest clients, your employees. Ask them the following question: "What is my unique, intrinsic value?" Have them respond with their answers via emails or texts and enter their answers based on the categories in the worksheet below. Once you've collected the feedback, look for repetitive words, synonyms, and recurring themes. Circle those key words and keep them close to you as we journey throughout the rest of this book together. Within these words lies your value proposition.

We all have the power to change people's lives. Do not underestimate this power, and do not be so precious with it. Give it away. Every day. Everywhere you can. For free, and infused with value.

Then witness how it all expands: your self-worth, your net worth, you.

YOUR UNIQUE
INTRINSIC VALUE

PERSONAL

PROFESSIONAL

OTHER

Be.

in service

Personal Branding starts not by making
everyone in the world care about you
but showing how much you care
about them instead.

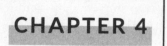

SO . . . WHAT IS PERSONAL BRANDING?

> "It takes courage to grow up
> and be who you really are."
>
> *e.e. cummings*

I'll be the first to admit that the concept of branding yourself is kinda weird.

Many people scratch their heads at the notion that they themselves are a *brand*. I get it.

How can you productize the human spirit? How can one thrust themself into the spotlight *without* appearing egotistical and self-important?

Well, my friend, here's the truth. You *are* important. You would not be here if you weren't. And I don't just mean *here* as in reading this book; I mean here on Earth. We all have an undeniable, utterly unique, unreplicable gift to share with the world. And the mere act of *sharing* it is the very reason you exist.

But, in the spirit of puns, let's *be real*: there are people who are doing this work very well, and far too many people who are not. It's a large part of why this industry is so misunderstood.

I am about to guide you, step-by-step, through the SimplyBe. methodology of how to build an authentic personal brand message and an expert strategy. You've already discovered the importance of embracing your shit, the heart of your value, and the necessity of generosity. It's time we level the playing field and set the record straight on the industry of personal branding itself.

It's time to redefine what it is—and what it isn't—once and for all. We're going to take a look at all the "myths" you potentially have about this space and debunk them one at a time.

FACT VERSUS FICTION

Our thoughts create our reality. We all have perceptions (and delusions) about what's true, and if it's true to *us*, then it must be fact. I respect that. So with loving, delicate, nonjudgmental hands, let's pick up each myth you potentially have about personal branding. We are going to examine perception versus reality; fact versus fiction; fear versus love. It is only when we open ourselves up to a new way of thinking that we can step into a new way of being.

Myth: A personal brand is a two-dimensional projection of what I want the world to know about me.

Truth: A personal brand is a 360-degree expression of who you are as a person, what you do as a professional, what makes you great at what you do, and what matters to you the most, along with your passions, your past, your perspective on both work and life, and your visions for the future. It's the story of your soul by design.

Myth: Personal branding is an act of vanity.

Truth: Building the brand called "you" is an act of service and therefore the most loving thing you can do for the world. We all have a unique value, and it is without question that what you know, do, and understand has the power to actually *help* another human being. Imagine a place where we all shine with confidence in ourselves in service of the greater collective. When we put our egos down and ask ourselves, "Who needs me? How can I serve?" This is love. This is personal branding done well and done correctly.

Myth: A personal brand is my Instagram channel.
Truth: Your personal brand is a platform for you to share your stories, lessons, wisdom, and truth, a.k.a. your thought leadership. Retweeting random shit and sharing memes all day does not a thought leader make. To boot, you do not own Instagram, Facebook, Twitter, or Snapchat. Mark Zuckerberg, Jack Dorsey, and Evan Spiegel do. What do *you* own? Your message. Your content. The intellectual property (IP) of your life's work. Your social media channels are places to share your IP and build a community, but your brand must exist beyond it. In fact, as you go forth to build your message, strategy, and platform in this book, you will see that social media is the very last place we arrive.

Myth: I don't have a presence online, so I don't have a personal brand.
Truth: You could very well have zero presence anywhere online, and you still very much have a personal brand. Why? Because by virtue of the fact that you're alive, you interface with other human beings offline. You know that place called the "real world"? Wherever you go, no matter who you are with or what you are doing, you are telling a story about yourself and leaving behind an impression. *Everything* is messaging. From the way you dress to the way you style your hair, walk into a room, shake hands, make eye contact, and make someone feel. It's *all* your brand. It lives offline as much as it does online. The more you become aware of your presence, the more you can own the image of how people perceive you. Building your personal brand offline not only becomes a key strategy for scaling your memorability but the ultimate act of self-empowerment.

Myth: My personal brand is the story I tell about myself.
Truth: Your personal brand is what other people say about you when

you're not around. The space between what *you* believe you are known for and what *other people* know you for is the gap this book is going to help you fill. You build your reputation with forward action. This means proactively, consistently, clearly, and constantly creating value for your clients, customers, and audience. You do this by way of content, such as blogs, videos, podcasts, newsletters, webinars, live events, workshops, retreats, programs, courses, and, yes, through a social media presence. It is then and only then that your personal brand becomes what you say it is. But if you are passive, it will become what others say, instead. You hold the pen, so write your own damn narrative.

Myth: Building a personal brand is a time suck.
Truth: Guess what? There are other people in the world who do what you do, who are targeting the same clients as you, who have similar dreams as you, who are getting the gigs you want. These people are not necessarily any better or worse than you at what you do. *The world just simply knows they exist.* Personal branding is a must-have in today's digital business world. It maximizes your reach and therefore maximizes your time. With the push of a button, you can reach another human on the other side of the planet. This didn't exist even fifteen years ago. Constant connectivity is a blessing for anyone with a dream. It's time to stop demonizing the internet and instead start honoring it and taking massive advantage of it. There is nothing more worthy of your time than your dreams.

Myth: Anyone can brand themselves as an "expert," which takes away my credibility.
Truth: We spend an awful lot of time comparing ourselves to other people, don't we? We spend even more time judging those people, and worse, judging ourselves. What if we lived in an ever-abundant universe where there was enough to go around and everyone had free will? Oh wait . . . *we do.* Who cares what other people are

doing? *Your* business is focusing on the endless possibilities that lie at your feet when you start owning, out loud, that you are, in fact, an expert. Just because someone else is saying it too doesn't take away from your legitimacy. We're going to study the power of PR in this book and how the PR industry has evolved since the dawn of the internet and the explosion of social media. Today, anyone can become a contributing writer for an established publication, start their own video series, build their own platform, and become perceived as influential. Are you going to tell me that's a bad thing? If so, that's just you playing small, my friend.

Myth: Authenticity is overused.
Truth: This is my favorite myth, and I understand why it exists. With the advent of the influencer, the rise of the Insta Story, and the behind-the-scenes content we have become so used to consuming, it's hard to tell the difference between what authenticity really is, and what it is pretending to be. Authenticity is unfiltered. It's unapologetic. It's honest. It doesn't have perfect lighting or the right hashtag mix. Authenticity doesn't have all the answers. Authenticity owns its imperfections. Authenticity takes responsibility when it makes mistakes. Authenticity shows up for its audience on the good days *and* the bad days.

Inauthenticity is the highlight reel. It's only part of the story; the part that makes everyone feel comfortable. Inauthenticity is the attempt to be, above all else, likeable. Perhaps most disturbingly, inauthenticity is showing up offline as a completely different person than the one you represent online.

With this book, you, my dear, hold in your hands the power to become a shining example of *real* authenticity. And for the record, I would like to *celebrate* the fact that authenticity is "overused"! Because if it is, that would mean more people are showing up in their full fucking light, power, and potential. What a world that would be.

It starts with you, simply being you. When you fully step into yourself and *share* yourself, you become not only a magnet for the opportunities you seek to grow your net worth but an example of awakening as well. Your freedom in simply being is permission for others to be themselves too. Something they have been waiting their whole lives for, and most of them don't even know yet. You get to be the eye opener. The game shifter. The world changer. And how do you *really* change the world? One person at a time.

Start the domino effect.

YOUR AUTHENTIC PERSONAL BRAND MANIFESTO

Before we move forward, I want you to take an honest look in the mirror. If we're about to go forward to build an authentic personal brand the *right* way, you must claim your place in the spotlight. In order to show up truly authentic, you must take every self-limiting belief that *you* have about this industry and smash the shit out of it.

In the box on the next page, I want you to list every fear you've felt that has held you back from building the platform called "you," every judgment you've ever quietly held about someone else in the spotlight, every lie you've told yourself about your worthiness to be known, and every myth you've ever had about personal branding. The more honest you are willing to be here, the more authentic your brand will ultimately become.

Then I want you to rewrite each fear-based statement looking through the lens of love in the box on page 42. I want you to reenvision each statement from the viewpoint of your worth: that you deserve to be seen, that there is enough abundance to go around, that there is a huge audience out there that needs you, and that when you win, other people win too. Make the choice that every dream you have ever dreamed will come true. Assume that it will. Know that it will. Go.

FEAR

LOVE

Example: if I share myself vulnerably online, my clients will feel even more connected to my work, and as a result, my business will grow.

Take a look at your love statements. This is your authentic personal brand manifesto. Come back to these beliefs as you read through the book to remind yourself of your worthiness to shine, to grow, to succeed, to Be.

With the courage and understanding you now have to Be. real, it's time to channel it into the endless opportunities that will unequivocally unfold when you decide to Be. your brand.

Just like that, you're right on time.

Authenticity is rebellion, and the world needs someone to lead the revolution. It's up to leaders, experts, authorities, change agents, and game changers to come together to lead with Love, Light and Service. It starts with you, simply being you.

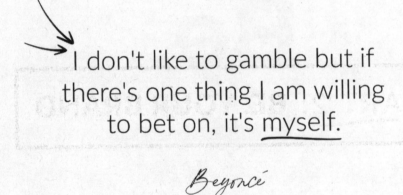

I don't like to gamble but if
there's one thing I am willing
to bet on, it's <u>myself</u>.

Beyoncé

PART 2: BE. YOUR BRAND

HOW TO PLAY THE (LONG) GAME

"You always have two choices.
Your <u>commitment</u> versus your fear."

I met Erica just after she moved from Boston to Chicago and had zero network and a job in real estate she hated. A supremely talented home chef with a passion for Chicago's food scene, she started a blog covering her favorite recipes and restaurants. The blog's initial primary objective was simply to keep her friends back in Boston informed on what was going on in her new life in this new city and to give herself a creative outlet.

After running the blog for a few months, she took the bold leap of quitting her real estate job to go full time on her dream of becoming a food blogger. She had a small readership at the time and an Instagram following of about five thousand people. As a way to make revenue, she hosted small cooking classes in her home and charged $40 a person—enough to cover food costs and make a small profit. To grow her brand, she made a concerted effort to go to every restaurant she could in order to build relationships with chefs and attend every foodie event to build her personal network, all while publishing a blog on her website every single week and growing her following on Instagram. She worked day in and day out, testing and learning her "business model," launching new services, partnering with different brands, making imperfect yet iterative and ever-evolving choices to grow her brand.

These tiny, micro, daily actions led to huge results. Today, Erica is a bona fide entrepreneur who runs a nationally recognized, full-time brand: EverythingErica. From this platform, she has consulted for some of the largest brands in the country on their social media strategies, launched an influencer marketing agency supporting up-and-coming bloggers, regularly appeared on TV segments as an expert on food and cooking, and organically grown her Instagram following to 130,000 plus followers with unprecedented engagement rates. As a result, her business reached six figures in revenue, which enabled her husband to leave his joyless day job to help her run the company.

What's most compellingly important to note regarding Erica's story is not the sheer success of it but *the time it took her to get there*. Would you like to know the span of time between the day I met Erica when she first started to where she is today?

Six years.

You know what happened during those six years?

Eighteen months of barely breaking even. A six-figure partnership that fell through in the eleventh hour. Chronic illness and autoimmune issues from all the stress and eventual burnout. Friends she considered her inner circle who got jealous of her success and intentionally cut her out. A massive algorithmic Instagram change, which took away her ability to reach her community and forced her to rebuild her entire business from the ground up. I could go on.

The long game isn't just filled with seconds, minutes, hours, days, weeks, months, and years. It's also filled with blood, sweat, and lots of fucking tears.

This story should not discourage you. Everyone is on their own time line and is dealt their own hand. Some people grind for years until they make it. Some people get lucky in a matter of weeks. But the reality is this: we live in an increasingly saturated world filled with noise, distractions, deterrents, and other people just like us, clamoring for the ever-elusive, most valuable commodity: attention. The only way to build a sustainable brand (and business) that stands out above the rest is to put in the hard work—and play the long game.

Perhaps what was most significant about Erica's choices throughout her rise to success was how she embraced the power of mentors, advisors, and community to keep herself on track to grow. I was one of them. If you want success like Erica's, in whatever industry you're in, you must follow what I call the "four Cs":

1. **Consistency**—picking your lanes (i.e., your content types, your social channels, your tactics) and staying the course versus jumping all over the place
2. **Constancy**—showing up for your brand, your business, and your audience daily, weekly, monthly, quarterly, year after year
3. **Clarity**—having an unmistakable, ownable, one-of-a-kind message and a crystal clear value proposition that you don't deviate from
4. **Commitment**—keeping at it when life knocks you down, especially when you bravely and boldly put yourself out there

This is how you compound the size, the reach, and the impact of your platform.

We are going to cover all of these elements of your personal brand message and strategy in this section, but for starters, we are going to begin with the fourth and most foundational of the Cs: commitment.

Before we do, let's play a quick game. I want you to take a serious look at a few of the most successful entrepreneurs, executives, influencers, public speakers, podcasters, and authors "everyone" knows. Make a short list of three to five well-known personal brands, right here and now and write them in the blanks below.

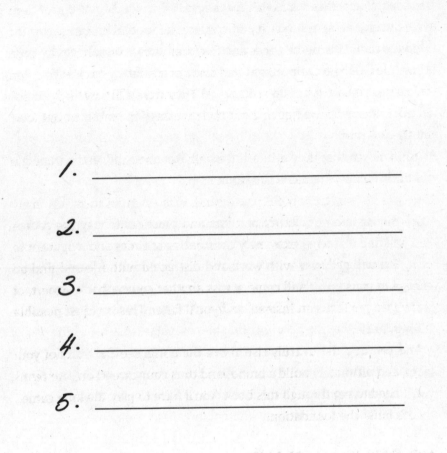

1. _____

2. _____

3. _____

4. _____

5. _____

Now, I don't want you to examine their current platforms. I want you to trace them back to where and when they started. Look them up on Instagram and scroll all the way down to the beginning of their feeds and look at the quality of content, as well as the engagement. Head to their Wikipedia pages and find their career history. Study their time lines. Google their images and find photos dating back to five, ten, twenty years ago. What do you notice? They were all most likely unpolished, imperfect, and figuring out their message in real time, out loud, on the internet.

You will see that they all started small. But above all, you will notice that they simply started and did not stop.

Before we can truly build your brand, it is essential to set up insurance through accountability partners and practices to stay the course. You will find this work extremely confronting at times and may want to quit. You will get busy with work and distracted with life and find an excuse to pause. You will come across another course, book, expert, or shiny thing to focus on instead, and you'll falter. This isn't just possible. It's inevitable.

And yet, in order to truly rise above the noise, see the fruits of your labor, and ultimately build a brand (and thus your career) on *your terms*, you'll need to get through this book. You'll have to play the long game.

Let's build the foundation.

NO ONE IS AN ISLAND

We live in a day and age where being a "hustler" is glorified and to be "self-made" is aspirational. We are bombarded with blatant imagery and subliminal messaging that celebrates the ideals of "crushing it," "slaying it," and "killing it." (Sounds painful.) Sure, to some degree, these sound bites can be motivational, but if we dig deeper into the true net effect of what the hustle culture is doing to our overall well-being (and chances for long-term success), the stats are staggering.

More than 60 percent of work absenteeism is attributed to psychological stress, and in a recent survey of two thousand employees, 40 percent said they were considering quitting their jobs because of the invisible disease called burnout.[1] According to a 2019 study by Deloitte, anxiety and stress have seen a 30 percent spike year after year since 2017 with no signs of slowing down.[2] With the rise of our dependence on technology and the ever-growing expectations to be constantly connected, we can only anticipate an even broader issue.

And yet, so many of us suffer in silence when we're overwhelmed, refuse to admit we're struggling in the first place, or don't ask for help.

What does this have to do with building a personal brand? In a word: everything.

No matter if you are the CEO of your business, an up-and-coming creative solopreneur, or a new employee looking to make a mark, the truth is this: we are all *humaning*.

Humaning is defined as "having human form or attributes susceptible to or representative of the sympathies and frailties of human nature." Read: life is hard; don't do it alone.

We enlist therapists, coaches, consultants, personal trainers, doctors, healers, assistants, and friends to help us get through our most challenging times and break through to the next level. Why wouldn't you enlist someone to help you build your most invaluable, essential business tool?

You can't scale a business without a team. You can't raise money without people who believe in your dream. You can't get the life-changing meeting of your dreams without someone else simply saying, yes. It takes a village to raise a family, build a home, launch a product, *and* become your brand.

Your business needs a support staff. So does your soul. Building a personal brand sits at the intersection of the two. And so, I would like you to take this moment to surrender to the fact that you are human. You are not an island. You're going to need some help. Own it and embrace it. It's time to find your running mate on your journey to Be.ing.

SHIT'S ABOUT TO GET REAL: MEET YOUR ACCOUNTABILITY PARTNER

A few years ago, as I was starting SimplyBe., I made a pact with my dear friend Daniel, who had been running an agency similar to mine for years. I was looking for guidance on how to scale my newly formed business, and he was looking for some tips on how to build his personal brand in service of his company. The pact was that we would become "co-mentors" and meet once a quarter for breakfast. The meetings were set at 8:00 a.m., so that we could end around 9:30 a.m. to start our workdays, and we always met at the same location. We took turns, each of us getting forty-five minutes to share and get feedback. Without fail, we met quarter after quarter for two years. To this day, I make business decisions on hiring, clients, and productizing using the wisdom he imparted. Daniel has since launched his own successful podcast, newsletter, and Instagram with the direction I gave him. This is the power of implementing accountability partners and structures.

My accountability partnership with Daniel contained two critical components:

1. Our meetings were mutually beneficial.
2. We made this commitment "official" by giving our meeting a name: the Co-Mentors Breakfast. This transformed what would typically be a nondescript meeting on our calendars into an actual pact.

The best way to stay committed is to find yourself a personal brand accountability partner. And the best way to ensure that accountability partner stays the course alongside you is to make it a win-win. Your accountability partner needs you as much as you need them.

Let's start by selecting your running mate. This person can be your spouse, your best friend, your favorite colleague, your business partner, or your mentor. The key is that you are both working on a clearly defined goal. This way, the partnership is equitable and energetically aligned.

To begin, use the checklist on the next page to identify at least three people in your life who would make a good fit.

- *You have a good understanding of each other's career history, current business, and future business goals.*

- *You have a deep understanding of each other as human beings: your talents, your motivations, what makes you "tick," and what you care about most.*

- *Your partner has a general understanding of the personal branding space and/or has zero judgments or stigmas regarding the power of building a personal brand.*

- *You both have a general understanding of each other's industry and are willing to stay open, ask questions, and add any value you can.*

- *You have regular or semiregular "access" to each other; meaning you can connect easily and effortlessly.*

- *You are willing and unafraid to call each other out on your shit and tell each other the truth.*

- *You believe in each other as much, if not more so, than you believe in yourself.*

- *You enjoy each other's company. (Because if it's not fun, then what's the point?)*

Then, with your three potential accountability partners in hand, use the accountability tracker on each of them to find the most qualified "candidate."

Once you've chosen your finalist, it's time to pick up the phone (or even better, schedule a Zoom date or take them out for coffee) and simply *ask*. Face-to-face conversations are always infinitely more powerful. If you're feeling a little nervous, use the "script" on page 56 as a guidepost to start this conversation.

YOUR ACCOUNTABILITY TRACKER

NAME			
They get YOU.			
They get your business.			
They understand the power and importance of personal branding.			
You get their industry and are willing to add value where you can.			
You have regular or semiregular "access" to each other.			
You are willing and unafraid to tell each other the truth.			
You believe in each other as much, if not more so, than you believe in yourself.			
You enjoy each other's company. (Because if it's not fun, then what's the point?)			

Thank you so much for taking the time to meet with me today. I value your time, as well as your presence in my life, which is the inspiration behind me reaching out. As part of my professional growth and personal discovery, I am embarking on the development of my personal brand to help me achieve my goals of X, Y, Z, by using the book Be. I am committed to following its methods and tools and, as a part of this process, I am looking for someone who can keep me accountable to finishing this book and completing all of its exercises and worksheets. Due to our deep connection/relationship/friendship, coupled with your belief in me and my dreams, I believe this someone is you. I am asking you to be my personal brand accountability partner over these next few weeks/months as I build my brand. In exchange, I am offering to become your accountability partner, to help you stay the course of whatever it is you're focusing on as you build your business and career too.

Once you and your accountability partner have mutually agreed to the journey, it's time to set up your structures. Now, most people are busy as hell. Including you. The last thing your accountability partnership should feel like is a burden. That's why it's essential to find a rhythm and flow that feels light and easy. Make this something you look forward to week to week, month to month.

Here's a tool to get you started, with inspiration for defining your "checkpoints," which are the ways you will stay in touch. Once you've defined the structure of your checkpoints, it's then time to create your "cadence," or how often you'll perform each of the checkpoints. Finally, you'll want to impart your "hacks." These are the sneaky but simple strategies designed to ensure you stay the course.

CHECKPOINTS	CADENCE	HACKS
A monthly coffee date before work: pick an especially beautiful, creative, lively and/or peaceful place to meet that nourishes your souls.	Daily Weekly Monthly Quarterly	Calendar invites with fun, personalized meeting names
Zoom dates: switch up your Zoom backgrounds to surprise and inspire each other!		Phone alarms and ring tones with inspiring, motivational music
A text each and every Monday at 9 a.m. with an inspirational quote from your favorite author, funny meme from your favorite IG account, an educational video or TEDx talk, or a motivating song		Rewards you gift each time you hit a milestone

YOU'VE GOT THIS

I want to tell you something.

I see you.

I know this work is hard. I understand the feeling of wanting immediate results. I relate to the feeling of wanting to do it all yourself. I see you because I've been you. So have thousands of people I have worked with. I get you, and you've got this. *We* have got this.

With me and your accountability partner by your side, it's time to define your message, craft your strategy, and build your platform. Profound fulfillment, professional recognition, unprecedented success, deep spiritual growth, a renewed confidence, and a life-affirming sense of purpose are waiting for you on the other side.

Are you ready to Be.?

Hell yes, you are.

Be.
committed

Massive success is simply a compilation of
daily micro-actions. Keep yourself
accountable to these daily acts with your
Accountability Partner. Consider it your
Personal Brand Insurance Policy.

CHAPTER 6

YOUR MESS(AGE) IS YOUR MAGIC

*"Clarity is momentum that
has no resistance in it."*

Abraham Hicks

A forewarning: not everyone will like this brand called you.
People certainly have not liked mine, and I have had to learn to accept that. Over the years, I have been told by my audience, followers, and clients that they love my affinity for bright yellow pineapples and incessant positivity. I have been told by others that they despise it or don't believe in it. I have been accused of wanting to be famous. I have been told my success and joy makes me "unrelatable." I have been criticized for being "too polished" and "too positive." I have been paralyzed by what other people think of me and settled into inaction because I allowed myself to believe it. I have had to work really, really hard to ignore the voices of the masses and listen to the sound of my heart instead. Step-by-step, day by day, one loving, worthy belief about myself at a time. Slowly but surely, I have risen out of the fear of judgment and into inspired action. If I can do it, anyone can.

This is the time your self-worth matters more than ever.

YOUR VIBE ATTRACTS YOUR TRIBE

I know I lamented earlier that no one cares about you. (Spoiler alert: it's still true.) But before we can get to building an external personal brand that is in service to your mission, your community, and company, we do need to *start* with you.

No one else has your unique blend of experiences based on your childhood, schooling, relationships, heartbreaks, failures, successes, travels, and career track, so you intrinsically possess something that literally NO ONE ELSE on the planet possesses. This is your message. This is the cornerstone of your brand. So, how do you actually define it?

We'll get there in a few.

First, let's remember that we are not building just any brand. We are building your personal brand, and you are a human, not a product, a logo, a company, or a website, and you're not a human *doing*. You are a real-life, breathing, feeling, dreaming, complicated human *being*.

The purpose of a brand is to create an emotional connection, memory, and lasting affinity within itself. People aren't trying to be brands; brands are trying to be people. This is good news for you. You *already* contain the magic sauce brands only *wish* they could possess: your *humanity*. Blend this invaluable asset with your professional, expert value, and you've got the ingredients for the most powerful type of "brand" available today:

You.

The more "you" that you are, the more polarizing you will become. That's because your vibe will attract your tribe. (As a Jewish woman, the word "tribe" has always resonated with me, given my heritage stems from the Twelve Tribes of Israel, and my faith is a huge part of my identity.) Now, this this isn't just a cheeky catch phrase but rather a personal affirmation I want you to make to your soul. Say it, right here, right now, out loud:

"My vibe will attract my tribe."

Your "vibe," a.k.a. your vibration, gets stronger, more compelling, more magnetic, and more powerful the more unapologetically authentic you become. As such, you are going to magnetize people who resonate with it and repel people who do not.

Newsflash: THIS. IS. AMAZING! When you emphatically draw your right people in *and* put off the ones who don't belong, it's a sign that you are doing this work right. And by "right" I mean *authentically.* You are building *your* tribe. And it's the only tribe you need to truly succeed.

As such, there's one major requirement as you walk the path to building a fully expressed, wholly authentic personal brand: you are going to have to stop giving a shit about what people think about you. You probably hear this a lot: from your friends, your life coach, your favorite famous person, and probably your mom.

I am telling you this as your business strategist.

Rising above the fear of others' perception of you as you build your personal brand is your number one key to being successful at this work. Consider the people you admire most for their ability to impact the world: entrepreneurs, innovators, influencers, and the world's greatest leaders. For me, it's Oprah, Ray Dalio, Gary Vaynerchuk, Simon Sinek, Rachel Cargle, Danielle LaPorte, Luvvie Ajayi Jones, Glennon Doyle, Lady Gaga, and RuPaul. Do you think any of them spend time worrying if people judged them for their ideas, their opinions, their outfits, their haircuts, their statements, or their choices?

Hell to the no!

They innately understand that being judged, disliked, misinterpreted, and misunderstood is part of the deal when one puts themselves boldly and bravely out into the world in order to make a difference. And in order to make a difference, you must be seen.

It's time to let *yourself* be fully seen. By the people who will "get it" and the people who might not.

It's time to simply be you. It's time to unleash your superpower.

BE. A LASER BEAM

In today's digital marketing era, most people are familiar with the adage, "Content is king."

This is bullshit. (Not to mention a recipe for overwhelm.)

People have been taught to believe that the more content you create online, the more visible you become. This philosophy applied at the dawn of social media, or what I like to call the "Wild West." Flashback to 2005-2007. YouTube had launched, Facebook had just expanded beyond universities, Twitter was all the rage, LinkedIn was desolate, and Instagram didn't even exist. To stand out and reach audiences at scale was pretty darn easy. It was such a wide open playing field that all you had to do was create content, and you were winning.

Let's demonstrate a very likely hypothetical of how it used to work when it came to creating organic content on the internet to scale your platform. It would go something like this:

It's 2007 and you share an elusive post in the Facebook feed about your recent breakup. BOOM! Every single one of your "friends" saw it, and half of them commented to commiserate and cheer you on.

It's 2008 and you go a bit rogue with a stream of fleeting thoughts on Twitter about why it's so tough to fund-raise as a female. HOLLER: the investor of your dreams sends you a direct message (DM) offering to take a look at your pitch deck.

It's 2009 and you whipped up a couple of hilarious Youtube videos of your dog chasing its tail. CONGRATULATIONS! You just went fucking viral.

You behaved like this online consistently and over the course of the next few years, you accrued a loyal following based on the mere fact that they *simply knew you existed*, not necessarily because you were adding any particular value to their lives.

Times have changed, my friend. You can't garner attention based on sheer volume or basic quantity. The mass of the internet itself has far outweighed your content creation whims. Today, you've got to get clear. I'm talking laser fucking sharp. You can't get away with an unclear online presence anymore. That's because you (and me, for that matter) are up against one vicious, unrelenting, ever-increasing, universal obstacle. It's called *noise*. And, it's only getting louder. Don't take it from me. The proof is in the pudding. Let's look at the following table to explore the noise I'm referring to and examine the growth of users across not only each platform but the whole damn internet from 2007 up until today.

CHANNEL	2007	TODAY
Facebook	20 million users	1.68 billion users[1]
YouTube	34 million users	2 billion users[2]
LinkedIn	10 million users	700 million users[3]
Twitter	6 million users	330 million users[4]
Instagram	0 users	1 billion users[5]
The whole freakin' internet	1.1 billion	4.48 billion[6]

Creating content just for the sake of it is a waste of time, not to mention ineffective. Today, the only way to cut through the noise is to have a laser-sharp brand message. Content lost its crown a while ago. Today, *clarity* is king, and consistency is queen. That's why it all starts here, with your crystal clear, unapologetically authentic personal brand message.

Let's pierce through.

YOU'RE A HOT MESS, JESS

I didn't always know what I was doing. There was a period of time where I thought the name of the game was to make noise, not cut through it.

I was launching SimplyBe. and wanted to position myself as *the* leader in personal branding. So I began creating a ton of content and implementing a bevy of tactics to get myself seen. I blogged every week on my website, sent out a weekly newsletter to my email list, and posted daily across all my social channels, including Facebook, Instagram, and Twitter. I was doing all the right things, or so I thought, and I was frankly feeling pretty damn good about myself.

A few months in, I went for coffee with my friend Mark, who definitely fits the criteria of an accountability partner. He understood my business, wanted me to succeed, and wasn't afraid to tell me the truth. We were talking shop, sipping almond lattes, and nibbling on gluten-free scones when Mark looked at me squarely across the table and said, "I know you're looking to be seen as a personal branding expert, Jess. But I gotta tell you . . . I've been following you online and you're all over the place."

"All over the place?" I furrowed my brow and blinked.

He continued. "One day you're blogging about personal branding tips, the next day you're talking about your favorite Chicago neighborhoods on Instagram, then you're sharing a newsletter on inspirational conferences, then it's a Facebook post about your dog, and then another blog about your latest trip to Europe."

I blinked again, swallowing the frog in my throat in an attempt to keep from exposing my bubbling anxiety over what might come out of his mouth next.

"If you want to be seen as *the* authority on personal branding, you've gotta *be about it*. Pick your lanes. Stay the course. That's how people will begin to see you as the thought leader I know you want to be. But right now, you're a hot mess, Jess."

While this was no doubt painful to receive in the moment, it was hands down one of the most powerful conversations I have ever had in my professional career. I left that coffee date with Mark with a white-hot fire in my belly. I was going to get myself fucking clear, and stat.

My first step was to ask myself, "What do I want to be known for?" Well that one was easy: personal branding. But I knew I could not *just* be about personal branding. For one, people would eventually get bored and annoyed and tune me out. On the flip side, I knew there was more to me than just what I did for a living. There were a lot of other things in my life that I could be about too. And so, I made a long list of all the topics I *could* talk about on my platform. Then I took a look at that list and asked myself these questions:

- *What do I want people to truly know me for?*
- *Do these topics enhance and elevate my professional expertise or detract from it?*
- *Do these things convey a full human story, not just a professional one?*
- *What is my true depth of knowledge and/or passion about each of these topics?*
- *Could I talk about these topics in the long term?*
- *What is sacred and private?*

I cross-referenced my answers to these questions against the list of topics I had come up with, and what I narrowed it all down to became my brand. Instead of a hot mess I started operating like a bona fide expert. And that's what I became.

What baffled me was how *simple* this was to do. Your brand is simply the story you tell about yourself. Over and over again. That's it! It's actually not that complicated to build an expert brand. You just need to be intentional, consistent, and laser sharp.

This newfound clarity in my brand message fueled my business beyond my wildest expectations. By walking my talk, I have scaled my business to seven figures in a few short years, doubling and tripling our revenue year after year, attracting top-tier talent to join my team, and working with ideal clients across the world.

It all came down to my brand message. It's now my trademarked methodology, and it's changing people's lives, not just their brands. And I'm going to teach you how to do this yourself. Right now.

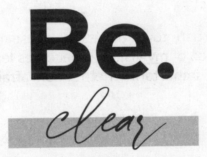

Be.
clear

The old adage of "Content is King" is dead. Clarity is King. It's not a matter of making a ton of noise. It's about cutting through the noise with a powerful brand message.

CHAPTER 7

INTRODUCING THE PERSONAL BRAND HOLOGRAM

"When I dare to be powerful, to use my strength in service of my vision, it becomes less and less important whether I am afraid."

Audre Lorde

Enter the Personal Brand Hologram. This is SimplyBe.'s registered trademarked framework I developed to crystalize clear and utterly unique brand platforms for my clients. This is the tool that I have used with all of my agency clients, taught to hundreds of workshop students, and shared with thousands of people at my speaking engagements. It's a tried-and-true formula that works for EVERYONE, no matter what you do or where you are in your personal branding journey.

Why do I call it a "hologram"? By definition, a hologram is "a three-dimensional image formed by the interference of light beams from a laser or other coherent light source."

As it relates to a personal brand, I have redefined the word to mean "a multidimensional being, come to life through the power of one's own inner light, coherently conveyed by beaming itself with laser-sharp clarity onto the world."

Humans are not two-dimensional frameworks written on a piece of paper. We are three-dimensional, deeply feeling, beautifully flawed, undeniably triumphant, complicated creatures walking through the world. Your Personal Brand Hologram will serve as the rock-solid foundation for a *clarified*, genuine, one-of-a-kind personal brand message that cuts through the noise and attracts a core tribe that not only appreciates your thought leadership but *needs* it in order to thrive.

PERSONAL BRAND HOLOGRAM FRAMEWORK

The Hologram contains three components:

1. Your Headline
2. Your four Brand Pillars
3. Your Unique Insights

Let's break each of its components down, one at a time.

THE PERSONAL
BRAND HOLOGRAM®

1 **BRAND PILLAR**

UNIQUF INSIGHTS

2 **BRAND PILLAR**

UNIQUE INSIGHTS

Headline

3 **BRAND PILLAR**

UNIQUE INSIGHTS

4 **BRAND PILLAR**

UNIQUE INSIGHTS

Your Headline

Your Headline is the all-encompassing, encapsulated definition of you. Think of it as your slogan. It can be a phrase, a word, a statement, a question, or even a symbol. It's the singular notion, the instantaneous thought you want people to think of when they hear your name and vice versa. Imagine your life was a book, and your name was the title of that book. Your headline would be the subtitle.

A forewarning about the Headline: it's the trickiest part of the Hologram and usually the last piece of the puzzle. I like to say that finding your perfect Headline is like finding your perfect apartment, your perfect city, or your perfect romantic partner. You have to try out a few before you find "the one." But when you do . . . you'll *just know*.

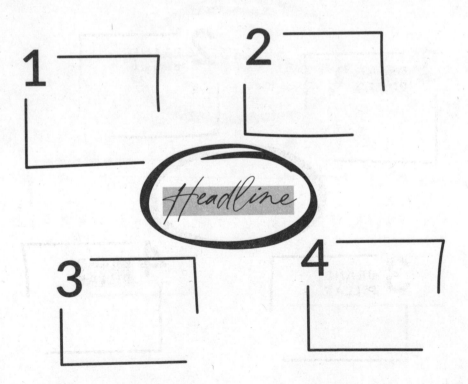

Your Four Brand Pillars

Next up, we've got your four Brand Pillars. Remember my coffee date with Mark? If you want to be seen as a thought leader, you cannot talk about twenty-five different things online and expect to be seen as a thought leader. If you do, you will come across like the hot mess that I was. By the same token, you can't just talk about the one thing you want to be seen as an expert in, e.g., real estate, law, fitness, travel, motherhood, design, cooking, tech, finance, personal branding, and so on. Do that, and you will become a downright snooze. You are more than what you *do*, yet you cannot share everything that you *are*. You must get selective and consider what you want people to truly know you for.

You might be asking, "Why four?" Because branding is an exercise in clarity. Four is the sweet spot, as it's small enough to achieve that clarity and large enough to demonstrate the breadth of your humanness.

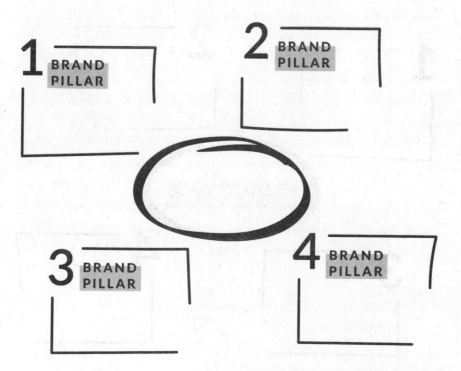

Start to make your list of potential Brand Pillars using the questions below as guidance. I recommend that you get out about eight to ten and then whittle them down to four from there.

- *What are the things I care the most about?*
- *What are the things I could talk about endlessly?*
- *What are the things that demonstrate my expertise and my humanity?*
- *Do these topics enhance and elevate my professional expertise or detract from it?*

Your Unique Insights

Once you have your four Brand Pillars defined, let's look at your Unique Insights.

This is where shit gets good.

So say you're a finance expert. That's cool. So are my dad, my husband, my CFO, and hundreds of thousands of other people who work in that industry. Perhaps you're an expert graphic designer. Awesome. I know thirty-two other graphic designers I could hire tomorrow. Personally, I consider myself a travel buff. So do millions of other millennial women on Instagram who look like me. Who actually cares? It's not that interesting, compelling, or unique to simply declare you are an expert in finance, design, or travel. This is about drilling into the specific nuances, beliefs, discretions, and points of view within each Brand Pillar that are unique to you based on your one-of-a-kind life experiences. Once you take the time to honor and clearly define these experiences, you and you alone own your brand. Put words to it, and that's where the magic happens. Take a look at your four Brand Pillars and ask yourself the following questions about each one:

- *What are your core beliefs around this topic?*
- *What are you against?*
- *What are your flaws?*
- *What have you learned about it?*

Once you've written your answers, pull out three to five phrases that you feel best define your position regarding this topic. These are your Unique Insights which are written within your four Brand Pillars. This is when your one-of-a-kind brand identity comes to life.

Now, let's take a look at how the Hologram manifests into form so that you can build yours.

A FAMOUS HOLOGRAM IN ACTION

Quick pulse check: Who is the most fun to follow on social media?

- *OwnNetwork or Oprah Winfrey?*
- *Virgin brands or Richard Branson?*
- *VaynerMedia or Gary Vaynerchuk?*
- *Endeavor or Bozoma Saint John?*
- *HuffPost or Arianna Huffington?*

I am going to assume you chose the latter on each one. At the end of the day, a consumer is going to choose to invest their time, money, and energy into one brand over another based on the emotional connection they feel to it. This is called brand affinity. A personal brand is the secret tool for establishing that connection. Oprah, Richard, Gary, Bozoma, and Arianna have clearly figured this out and have exploited their own personal brands brilliantly in service of their organizations.

For exploration's sake, let's take a deeper look at one of these famous leaders who clearly figured out this strategy.

Oprah Winfrey: Super Soul

When you hear the name Oprah, what word or phrase comes to mind? Perhaps its *queen* or *Midas touch* or *inspiration* or *mogul*. But if you think about the word or concept that is synonymous with Oprah Winfrey, the word *SuperSoul* undeniably comes to mind. The term literally and consistently comes to life on her platform in a multitude of places: *SuperSoul Sunday*, the *SuperSoul Conversations* podcast, the SuperSoul100 list. It's also the *essence* of her message.

OPRAH'S PERSONAL
BRAND HOLOGRAM®

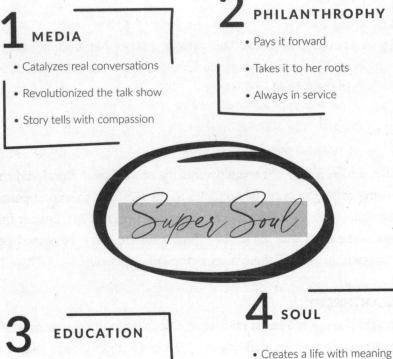

1 MEDIA

- Catalyzes real conversations
- Revolutionized the talk show
- Story tells with compassion

2 PHILANTHROPHY

- Pays it forward
- Takes it to her roots
- Always in service

Super Soul

3 EDUCATION

- Provokes personal awareness
- Emphasizes self-reliance
- Promotes upward mobility

4 SOUL

- Creates a life with meaning
- Follow your divine path
- The ultimate unifier

Let's consider her four Brand Pillars, which I boiled down to the following:

1. **Media** (her true expertise and what put her on the map as a mogul)
2. **Philanthropy** (a key aspect of her business model and life's work)
3. **Education** (the format and through line in everything she creates)
4. **Soul** (her own personal why, and what she's trying to inspire in others)

As we explore her pillars, I'm going to extract her Unique Insights by emphasizing the most ownable components of her story, which are italicized in the following sections.

MEDIA

The Oprah Winfrey Show was the first of its kind in the world of talk shows, and as a result, it *revolutionized the entire format*. Oprah did this by being willing to bring taboo topics to the forefront that most people were afraid to discuss, thereby *catalyzing real conversations*. But her true magic came from *how* she probed these subjects and empowered people to open up and tell their stories: *through compassion*.

PHILANTHROPY

Although she is a self-made billionaire, Oprah has never forgotten where she came from and has made *paying it forward* a priority. She's *taken it to her roots* by establishing the Oprah Winfrey Leadership Academy for Girls in South Africa as one of her primary philanthropic initiatives.[1] And no matter what she's putting her name on, whether it's a book, a person, or her latest venture—just look at WW (Weight Watchers)—it's *always in service* of helping her community live their best and most fulfilling lives.

EDUCATION

Based on her own journey to success and financial independence, Oprah clearly believes in the power of education, not only as *a path to upward mobility* but as an opportunity to *provoke self-awareness*. Whether it's on her TV network, on her podcast, or at her live events, she continually empowers her audience to learn to trust and *rely on themselves* through educating themselves.

SOUL

Clearly Oprah's "why" is *to create a life with meaning by following your own path and using your soul to unite with others*, because no matter what you believe in, everyone has a soul.

See how easy and fun this is? It simply starts with intentional discretion in selecting four topics (what do you want to be truly known for and how does this ladder up to your business *and* humanity) and drilling down into the details of your career and personal story from there.

Want to see a real live Personal Brand Hologram? Here's mine to help inspire yours.

JESSICA'S HOLOGRAM

When I set out to launch SimplyBe., I was clear that I wanted to be seen as *the* personal branding expert. (Trust me, you have to go after what you want. No one is going to do it for you.) But my message was anything *but* clear. Mark was right: I was a hot fucking mess on the internet. Truth be told, I created the Personal Brand Hologram for me. It was the solution to my own disaster.

I first had to drill into what I *wanted* people to know and understand about my business, as well as about me, Jessica, the human being behind it. As I dug into my own message, I realized there were things I wanted my audience and clients to understand about me, including my entrepreneurial savvy, my expertise, my love for travel, and my spirituality and things that I didn't necessarily *need* them to know about like my marriage, my autoimmune issues, my love for fashion, and so on. Why?

For starters, I am not an expert in autoimmune diseases, I am not trying to be a fashion blogger, and my relationship with my husband is sacred and private. Second, this is about intentionality *and* discretion. This is the most beautiful part of this work: we get to choose our own

JESSICA'S PERSONAL BRAND HOLOGRAM®

1 FEMALE ENTREPRENEUR

- Lead with femininity, love, empathy, and kindness
- Masculine business savvy
- Walks the talk

2 AUTHENTIC PERSONAL BRANDING

- It's a necessity, not a nice-to-have
- Authenticity is your superpower
- Embrace your shit

3 EXPANSIVE ENERGY

- Travel expands my mind
- Move my body to move my soul
- Wellspring of positivity

4 SPIRITUALITY

- Connected to a deeper purpose
- Your vibe attracts your tribe
- The ultimate empath

narrative. When you blend your professional work with key aspects of your humanity, you still achieve authenticity without blurring your message. Let's dive in.

FEMALE ENTREPRENEUR

First and foremost, I am a female entrepreneur. So this is my first pillar. In many ways, business is a masculine pursuit. And yet I have chosen to run my business with *femininity, love, empathy, and kindness*. But what makes me different is that I can effortlessly shift between the feminine side of how I run my business and the *masculine savvy* required to do so in order to get shit done. I get a charge from being assertive and quick thinking, taking massive action, and problem solving. But what I am most proud of, and what I want people to know about my company, is that my team is predominantly made up of women, and I get a thrill out of "growing" them. I *walk my talk* by creating new female leaders in the world.

AUTHENTIC PERSONAL BRANDING

Moving on to my second pillar, which is authentic personal branding. There are a lot of other people who call themselves experts in this space. I know because I follow their work and find them truly inspiring. But I had to ask myself, "What makes me different?" I decided to boldly claim that building your personal brand is no longer *a nice-to-have but a necessity* if you want to win in business. I am transforming the perception of personal branding by reminding anyone who comes across my work that their *authenticity is a superpower* and that in order to truly connect with your audience, clients, and customers, you must first *embrace your shit*.

EXPANSIVE ENERGY

Traveling is also a huge part of my life. I have been to over thirty-five countries in the past five years alone. Sure, I love a luxury boutique hotel, a local modern art museum, and a sexy wine bar as much as the next gal, but what I love most about travel is how it humbles me and makes me feel so fucking small. *I love to travel because it expands my mind.*

Fitness is another way I express energy. I work out on a regular basis, but it's no longer to burn calories like I used to in my twenties and early thirties when my body dysmorphia dictated my every decision. Today, I move my physical body to move through my feelings, clear my head, release my emotions, and remove blockages. *I move my body to move my soul.*

And I make the daily choice to look at life with the glass half full. Especially, and most importantly, on the dark days. (Sometimes I need to have a meltdown first.) But I ultimately end up making the choice to be a *wellspring of positivity*. I do this for my team, my clients, and my community. I am cognizant that how I show up as a leader energetically impacts everyone around me. It's been this expansive energy, my third pillar, that has allowed me to bring my whole, truest, and healthiest self to my work and the world.

SPIRITUALITY

My fourth pillar is my relationship with spirit, which is the most important relationship in my life. I was raised Jewish but actually found God for the first time at eighteen years old, standing on a mountaintop in Ireland right after my deceased grandmother's spirit spoke to me in a Catholic chapel a few miles away. Since that time, I have opened up my view to faith and religion of all kinds and have adopted a plethora of beliefs from Buddhism, Hinduism, Taoism, Christianity, Judaism, and extraterrestrial theories and have blended them into my own experience of "God," "Source," "Light," "the Universe," insert whatever you want to call it. I have come to realize that connecting to any version of God allows you to *connect to a deeper purpose*. This is the essence of SimplyBe. I also have found that the more open I am about this part of my life publically, *the more this vibe attracts my tribe*, a.k.a. the right clients, employees, partners, and friends. Being connected to Source has required me to become ever more in touch with my emotions, and I use *my ultimate empathy* as a superpower to be in service of everyone I work with.

As for my headline, it's obviously SimplyBe. It's more than just my business name. It's the feeling, the experience, the story, and the statement I want people to think of when they hear my name. It's absolutely the all-encompassing, ever-encapsulating definition of Jessica Zweig. Staying true to my narrative authentically, clearly, and consistently with the Hologram has not only increased my sense of worth but has driven more of my right clients, employees, and network, impacting my success beyond my wildest expectations.

The Hologram is powerful. There is power in Light.

YOUR PERSONAL BRAND HOLOGRAM

Remembering that clarity is king, use the worksheet below to take all that you have unpacked about your truth, your greatness, your expertise, your humanity, and your *beingness*. Combine it with your newfound understanding of how great personal brands are architected to build your own Personal Brand Hologram.

Your Hologram is the foundation of this work. Keep it top of mind and close to your heart as you go throughout the rest of this book.

It's time, my friend. It's time to step into your Light.

Let it flow.

YOUR PERSONAL
BRAND HOLOGRAM®

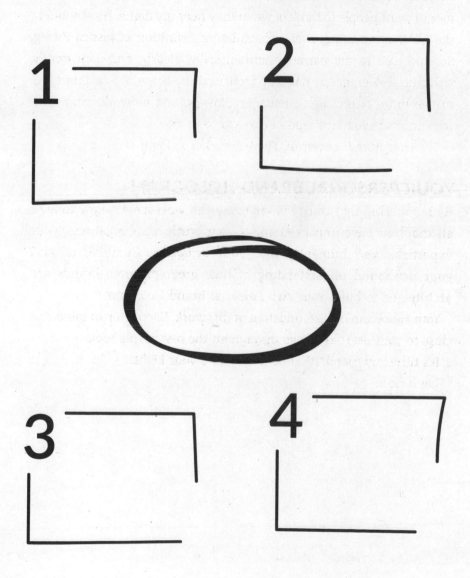

Be.
you

No one on the planet has your unique imprint,
experiences, perspective, and DNA. This is your
gift. Your genius. This is your personal brand.
And like the Hologram you are, it's your
responsibility to shine brightly, boldly, and
bravely as you move through the world.

CHAPTER 8

CREATE ENDLESS CONTENT WITH THE SUPERNOVA

"It is not in the stars to hold
our destiny, but In ourselves."

William Shakespeare

Content lost its crown years ago. With clarity as the new king of the internet, we need to address its royal, loyal queen: *consistency*.

This is one of the most essential principles of personal brand building. Your brand is simply what you say about yourself over and over and over again. Knowing your message is the first step. Reinforcing that message is the second. Do this enough, and watch how your brand transforms. There is deep power in consistency.

Consistency is what establishes reputation. You can't expect to give a single keynote talk on your area of expertise, say, sustainable urban living, and suddenly be known as *the* sustainable urban living guy or gal. But give a dozen talks on the topic, and you're an expert. Give a few dozen, and you're the authority. Leverage your talks for public appearances, podcast interviews, and a blog series, and you become the thought leader.

Consistency allows you to be taken seriously by your audience, your peers, your potential clients, and the media. It makes you recent and relevant. Consistency makes you legit in a world full of hacks.

Think about some of the personal brands you know and love. You can associate them with a clear brand story, not only because of *what* they say but also *how often* they say it.

An amazing example of consistency (and powerful personal brand building in general) is Arianna Huffington. Her authentic message was born from one singular defining moment. On April 6, 2007, during the height of Huffington Post's growth, she collapsed from sleep deprivation and exhaustion, broke her cheekbone, and woke up in a pool of blood. It was a day that she says "eternally changed her life."[1] This moment set her on a path to bring to light the importance of sleep and well-being, particularly in our current success-obsessed, always-connected work culture.

Now take a minute and go look at each of Arianna's social channels, search for her in Apple Podcasts to find her podcast interviews, check out all of her business platforms, look up the books she's written, *Thrive* and *The Sleep Revolution*, or simply google her name. You will find that every single touchpoint on her platform points to the same unmistakable, ownable, clarified message and mission: ending the burnout epidemic through the power of sleep.

Arianna Huffington is a powerful case study in personal branding, the SimplyBe. way. It started with the willingness to embrace her own shit, followed by a desire to be in service of the world around her, and then getting clear on her message. But it has been her *consistency* in sharing herself that has transformed her into a true thought leader.

With all due respect to Arianna Huffington, she is just a person, like you and me. Yes, she is someone who happened to have gotten clear on her passion and her gifts and had the courage to share them. But she is not superhuman. Becoming known in your field as the thought leader is not rocket science. If she can do it, you can too.

It's important that you remember this essential fact as we journey throughout the rest of this book together: you are worthy of sharing *your* message. You are not me and you are not Arianna Huffington. You're *you*. That's YOUR fucking superpower.

Now let's get consistent with it.

WHEN 1 + 1 = 3

So, assuming you love your Headline as much as you love your most favorite apartment *ever*, have developed Brand Pillars that reflect your expertise *and* your humanity, and have defined Unique Insights that convey a one-of-a-kind brand positioning, the natural question is, "What do I actually *do* with this thing?" Well, you could take each one of your Unique Insights and turn it into a respective blog piece or a podcast episode or inspiration for a keynote talk. While that certainly would work well in theory, it's extremely limiting to look at the Hologram that way. Why? Let's do some basic math.

There are four pillars in your Hologram, with roughly three Unique Insights per pillar. That's 4 x 3 = 12. Do you think twelve topics is enough to sustain an ongoing, endless array of topics for months, if not years on end, as you walk the ever-evolving, limitless path to thought leadership? Nope.

Before you freak out and think you're screwed, let's explore how you become truly limitless with your content.

First of all, your Personal Brand Hologram is a foundation. It's a starting point. If you only created content based on what was in your Hologram alone, you would eventually hit a wall. The next step is figuring out where it all connects, or rather, *collides*. When you combine your Hologram pillars and Unique Insights, you suddenly have an endless amount of content themes, topics, and titles that you could use for years on end, and that are completely unique to you.

These themes and topics will make their way into your blog, your podcast, your keynote talks, your social media posts, your bios, your LinkedIn summary, and even the way you speak about yourself at a meeting or a networking event. This is a critical and transformative part of your personal branding process, as it provides you with an endless supply of fresh, new, original ideas while preventing you from losing focus.

Buckle up. Things are about to explode.

INTRODUCING THE SUPERNOVA

By definition, a supernova is a star that suddenly increases greatly in brightness because of a catastrophic explosion that ejects most of its mass. (Thanks, NASA.)

At SimplyBe., we like to say that our clients are the stars, we are the catastrophic explosion, and together, we drastically and suddenly increase their brightness through a mass release of clear and consistent content.

Let's take a look at how the Hologram framework morphs itself into the brilliant, the sparkling, the flashing, the dynamic, the explosive *Superrrrnovaaaa!*

Actually it's just a Venn diagram.

(Sorry not sorry if that was a buzzkill.)

Nonetheless, the Supernova is a super powerful framework that will no doubt accelerate all of your content, allowing you to create days' worth of new topics while never losing that essential crystal clarity. Remember, consistency plus clarity equals memorability. And the personal brands that get remembered are the ones who get the opportunities, the clients, the open doors. That's why the Supernova is pure magic.

So let's blast off, shall we?

First, we will explore the function of the Supernova framework itself. It's essential that you understand how the tool is intended to be used in order to expand your brand content, before you dive into the exercise of building yours out.

Then, I'll take you into a Supernova "warm-up" to identify content themes to help get your creative juices flowing. These themes will be the springboard to your entire (endless) Supernova.

Finally, we will examine the intersection of your pillars by combining your content themes into specific titles and topics that will become the basis of all your future content.

For guidance and inspiration, I will be sharing my Supernova as a case study along the way so that you can bring yours to life even more effectively.

For now, please meet your cosmic, seismic awakening.

THE PERSONAL BRAND SUPERNOVA™

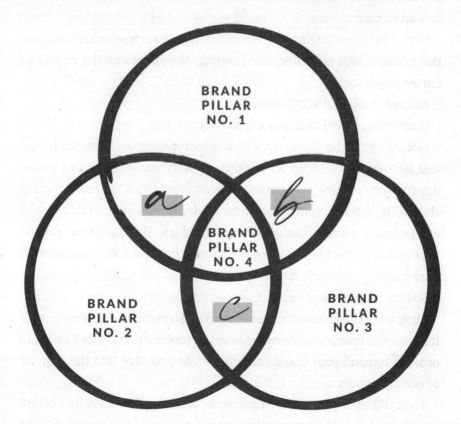

THE SUPERNOVA FRAMEWORK

To get started, you will be populating three of your four pillars in the three main sections of the Supernova (see figure below). The focus here is at the intersections, "A", "B," and "C," where your content topics and titles are born. You will see that a fourth pillar sits at the center of the Supernova—the intersection of your entire brand message. Your fourth pillar is your essence, your brand voice, the *feeling* that weaves its way into all of your content, regardless of the specific topic.

Let's recall the four pillars of my Hologram: (1) female entrepreneur, (2) authentic personal branding, (3) expansive energy, and (4) spirituality. I do not blatantly, explicitly talk about spirituality all day, every day. I am not an expert in spirituality, nor do I want to be seen as one. Instead I focus my core content on my first, second, and third pillars. However, my fourth pillar of spirituality includes empathy, purpose, and passion. This becomes my brand voice, which emanates within and throughout all of my communication. Therefore, your fourth pillar sits in the center of the Supernova.

Now look at your Hologram as you begin to prepare your Supernova. Decide which of your four Brand Pillars is closest to your "brand voice." That pillar will sit at the center of your Supernova.

Warm-Up

Using the warm-up worksheet on the next page, identify the Brand Pillars that tell the story of your professional expertise and unique value (remembering that your fourth pillar sits at the center of the Supernova as your brand essence). Populate these three pillars above the numbers 1, 2, and 3 on the worksheet, in no particular order.

When you look at your three pillars, what *new* words, insinuations, meanings, synonyms, like-minded ideas, and feelings come to mind? For example, perhaps one of your pillars is finance. Some related ideas that come to mind are money, wealth, stocks, economy, budgeting, spending, saving, investing, and so on.

Take a look at my Supernova warm-up for some inspo!

THE SUPERNOVA™ WARM-UP

BRAND PILLAR NO. 1	BRAND PILLAR NO. 2	BRAND PILLAR NO. 3
_____	_____	_____
_____	_____	_____
_____	_____	_____
_____	_____	_____
_____	_____	_____
_____	_____	_____

JESSICA'S SUPERNOVA™ WARM-UP

FEMALE ENTREPRENEUR	AUTHENTIC PERSONAL BRANDING	EXPANSIVE ENERGY
Women	Real	Light
Empowerment	Vulnerable	Fun
Birth	Growth	Power
Innovation	Own It	Movement
Fierce	Honest	Travel
Feminine	Transformation	Abundance
Team Building	Service	Explosion
Boss	Platform	Electric
Leadership	Expert	Vibrant
Brave	Thought Leadership	Charged Up
Business	Value	Amped
	True	Positivity
	SimplyBe.	Current

Now, going next to the "Supernova Warm-Up" worksheet on the previous page, open up your inner thesaurus and write your laundry list of like-minded words for each pillar. The key here is to follow your gut, not to limit (or judge) yourself, and write down anything and everything that comes to mind.

These become your content *themes*.

Once you've done this, you should be officially warmed up and ready to dive into the development of your unique (and endless) content.

The Intersections

This is where the shit gets good: at the intersection of these three pillars. You will take your above themes from columns 1, 2, and 3 and start to combine them together within spaces a, b, and c (see figure below) to create original topics.

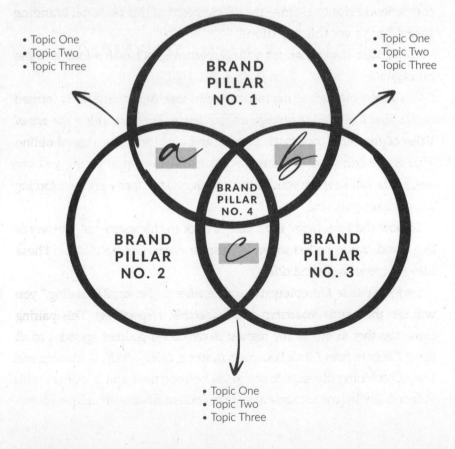

- Topic One
- Topic Two
- Topic Three

- Topic One
- Topic Two
- Topic Three

BRAND PILLAR NO. 1

a

b

BRAND PILLAR NO. 4

BRAND PILLAR NO. 2

c

BRAND PILLAR NO. 3

- Topic One
- Topic Two
- Topic Three

For the purposes of this exercise, aim for three to four unique topics within a, b, and c as your starting point, knowing that the possibilities here are truly unlimited. Push yourself. Don't make excuses. Quit the self-limiting belief that you are not a writer or a branding expert. You're not expected to be. You are you. And no one knows your experience, perspectives, and stories better than you do.

Consider the following examples: You can clearly see how your passion for travel has widened your perspective and has made you a better leader. Or how your fitness routine has spilled into your motivation for success at work. Or how your spiritual practice has improved your parenting skills. Or how your affinity for your favorite charity enhances your empathy with your clients. These are "combinations" of the differing aspects of yourself (and your brand) that can seamlessly be extracted into a specific topic that has value for someone else to glean—the whole point of this personal branding game! You've got this, my friend.

For further inspiration for your Supernova, let's take a look at mine on page 92.

You'll see how each of my pillars comes together to birth fully formed topics that I've used to engage my audience. Fun fact: these are *actual* titles of my blogs, podcasts, videos, and emails I have shared online. This is the beauty of the Supernova! It can inform anything you create, while still keeping you on track with crystal clarity and reinforcing what makes you, *you*.

So how did I get here? Let's take it back to the warm-up. The words I've listed, when paired together, inspire actual concrete ideas. These ideas become *topics* and *titles*.

Under "Female Entrepreneur" and "Authentic Personal Branding," you will see the words *leadership* and *vulnerable*, respectively. This pairing came together in one of my highest downloaded podcast episodes of all time: *7 Lessons from 7 Rock Bottoms in Business, Money, Body, Leadership, and Love*. Combining my experience as an entrepreneur and a woman with vulnerability led me to create a piece of content filled with unique value.

JESSICA'S SUPERNOVA™

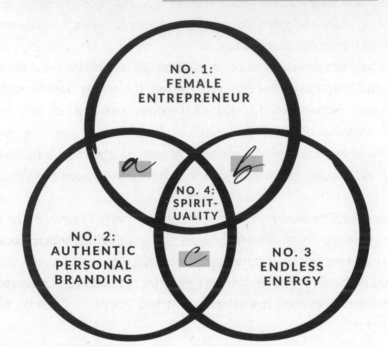

INTERSECTION A:
FEMALE ENTREPRENEUR + AUTHENTIC PERSONAL BRANDING

- 7 Lessons From 7 Rock Bottoms in Business, Money, Body, Leadership, and Love
- How to Crush Imposter Syndrome and Become an In-Demand Speaker
- Why Branding Yourself Isn't Vanity But a Responsibility

INTERSECTION B:
FEMALE ENTREPRENEUR + ENDLESS ENERGY

- Why Women Who Lift You Up Will Change Your Life
- Teams Built on Trust Have Exponential Power
- The Best Thing I Did to Scale My Business: Create More Female Leaders
- Connect Online with Positive Vibes to Grow Your Network IRL

INTERSECTION C:
AUTHENTIC PERSONAL BRANDING +ENDLESS ENERGY

- How to Use Your Vulnerability to Go Viral Online
- How My Ayahuasca Experience in Costa Rica Showed Me a New Layer of My Authenticity
- How Global Masterminds Transformed My Life, and How They'll Change Yours Too

Under "Female Entrepreneur" and "Endless Energy," you will see the words *team building* and *power*, respectively. Put those two concepts together, and you've got a blog called *Teams Built on Trust Have Exponential Power*. See how *easy* this can be?

For fun, let's do it one more time. Under "Authentic Personal Branding" and "Expansive Energy," you will see the words *transformation* and *travel*, respectively. I combined these two passions not only into an international Mastermind series I produced a few years ago and presented in Bali, Costa Rica, and Italy, but I also wrote a blog about it called *How Global Masterminds Transformed My Life, and How They'll Change Yours Too*.

I cannot tell you how many people I meet who tell me they just aren't creative and that they could never come up with enough stories to write a blog or launch a video series or start a podcast. I respond by saying, "Your life is stories. You have experienced millions of moments. Glean them. They contain wisdom unmatched. They hold the stars. You are infinite."

SHINE BRIGHT, MY FRIEND

The time has come. Strap on your seatbelt in your proverbial rocket ship, take a deep breath, and trust yourself. Grab a pen, and using the earlier warm-up worksheet along with the worksheet below, build your own Supernova.

Once you have completed the worksheet, keep it close. We will be revisiting these topics in the following chapters as we take your brand to the market, both online and off, using a personal brand strategy to reach the masses.

Yes, I said "the masses," because the masses need your light. Let yourself shine like the star that you are.

YOUR PERSONAL
BRAND SUPERNOVA™

_____   _____
_____   _____
_____   _____

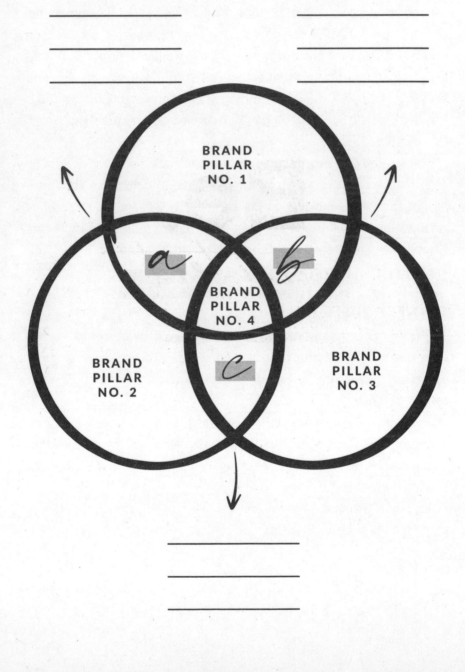

BRAND
PILLAR
NO. 1

a   *b*

BRAND
PILLAR
NO. 4

BRAND   BRAND
PILLAR   *c*   PILLAR
NO. 2   NO. 3

_____
_____
_____

Be.

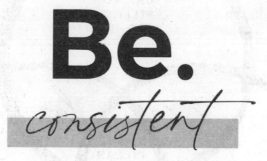

consistent

If clarity is king, consistency is queen,
and the key to your memorability.

CHAPTER 9

IT'S ALL BEEN SAID BEFORE

"Competition is always a <u>good thing</u>, it forces us to do our best while a monopoly renders people complacent and satisfied with mediocrity."

Nancy Pearcey

I'll never forget the time a friend of mine compared me to Marie Forleo.

I was 20 percent flattered, 75 percent self-conscious, 5 percent angry. Flattered for obvious reasons. Marie Forleo is a self-made multimillion-aire entrepreneur who's helped hundreds of thousands of women across the globe grow their online businesses. She's a *New York Times* bestseller, she has Richard Branson for a buddy, and she has graced Oprah's stage.

My self-consciousness said, "*Me?* No fucking way. I could never be that. And because I'm not that, and probably never will be that, I feel even smaller right now."

My anger was self-directed. I was *pissed* that I could never be Marie Forleo. I was *pissed* that I wasn't smart enough, savvy enough, pretty enough, well-timed enough, or connected enough to be her.

"Thanks . . . ?" I said to my friend.

Internally I said, "Screw you."

I got to a point in my career where I realized that I was right. I would never be like Marie Forleo (or Gabby Bernstein or Danielle LaPorte or

Brené Brown or Glennon Doyle or Liz Gilbert for that matter). And the fact that I was never going to be wasn't a tragedy. It was a miracle. You see, they weren't any better than me. They were them. And I am me. When I started fully accepting my own gifts, embracing my own unique path, and honoring my own precious dreams, the competition dissolved. The word literally lost its meaning.

Today, I am 100 percent confident in the brand, the business, and the platform called Jessica Zweig. Today, when I get compared to any successful woman, I feel gratitude filling my heart instead of feeling my face on fire.

This evolution of self-acceptance didn't happen overnight. It took me years to finally lay down my self-directed swords anytime I looked at another woman in my space. It took me calling bullshit on my imposter syndrome, rewriting my own self-limiting beliefs, diffusing the comparison game, and flipping my FOMO (fear of missing out) into what I call "JOWOW" (joy of watching others win). It took me realizing that when you mine the field of competition with an open and humble heart, there is *gold* to be found in the form of inspiration. I learned how to apply my inspiration into strategic choices that would ultimately refine what makes me different.

Let me show you how you can too.

WHITE SPACE

Welcome to what I like to call "brand positioning." It's literally defined as "how you promote yourself in the market." Now that you've got your signature themes for consistency and crafted quippy titles that align with your voice, expertise, and humanity from your Supernova, the next step is to develop your strategy. But before you can take yourself to market, build your credibility, amass followers by the thousands, and get paid top dollar for your work, you need to learn how to *actually* stand out among the competition like a singular shooting star against a pitch black sky.

Well, my little sparkler, there's one final step you must take before you blast out into the personal brand universe:

You've got to understand the other stars around you. Particularly the stars that look a lot like you do.

It's time to examine the competitive landscape. But let me first say this: I don't believe in competition. That word has a negative charge and induces an illness called the "comparison game." Don't let yourself go there like I did all those years ago. It's nothing more than a waste of energy. The point here isn't to stack chips and see who's got more. That's a zero-sum game. The point here is to be inspired by talented, successful, brave people in your space, in order to strategically explore what makes you different.

So while we will be referring to these personal brands as your "competition" for the purpose of this exploration, let's agree to remove the negative energetic trigger that comes with it. There is tremendous value in understanding not only people who are in your space but those who you admire. We want to name exactly what it is about them that we like, what we might not, and what we want to do differently. It won't matter how crystalized, clarified, and consistent you are if no one sees you. This is why you have to intimately understand where you fit in the sea of like-minded personal brands to stand out that much more. This is the final step in setting your brand identity up for success, before we dive into the strategy.

As much as we all hate to admit it, so much of the shit you want to say has been said before. The problem with the internet today is saturation. That's the bad news. The good news is that with so many people online promoting themselves using every platform out there to do so, inspiration for your differentiation is everywhere you look.

A forewarning: we all know the expression, "Imitation is the highest form of flattery." However, imitation is lame. It's annoying at best, and downright illegal at worst. The point of studying your landscape is not to rip people off. Quite the opposite. This work requires diving into the strategic choices and creative nuances your "competition" is making, and then . . . deviating.

This is a practice of *observing* your competitors, *processing* what is working for them (and what isn't), and *developing* new and informed strategic choices that are unique to you. Your competition should empower you to be that much more original.

I call this "finding the white space." White space is your blank canvas. It's the quiet stillness amid the noise. It's the unclaimed territory. It's your crystal clear sky. Your blue ocean. White space is an endless possibility. It's your miracle.

And there's always white space.

DOWN THE RABBIT HOLE

Before you can crystalize your originality, it's time to consider *who* you are competing with in the first place. It's important to choose comparable people in your space who represent attainable reach and credibility that you want to achieve within the next year. Read: if you have zero presence online, don't compare yourself to Kim Kardashian. If you are a first-time CEO building your very first company of five employees, don't use Bill Gates. That being said, it's important to pick a range of thought leaders who embody different attributes, and who all have established platforms. I like to pick three other personal brands. It's the sweet spot for understanding various mediums, strategies, tactics, visuals, PR plays, and tone without overwhelming yourself.

When it comes to selecting your three competitors, you might already have a few key people in mind. Perhaps they are the people you have admired for years. That's a great starting point, but I challenge you to view the landscape more finely and discover new people you've never heard of before.

A great place to go down the personal-brand-landscape rabbit hole is . . . Google. (I know, shocker). I would also look to Instagram, which has quickly become a top search engine in its own right, and where most personal brands market themselves today to one billion users. A good rule of thumb: if you're in any sort of creative or lifestyle industry (wellness, beauty, fashion, coaching, food, design, relationships, travel, entertainment), start with Instagram. If your industry relates to more mainstream business (finance, real estate, media, technology, venture capital, publishing, software, manufacturing, or anything B2B), head to Google.

Say you're in wellness. A great starting point would be to search Instagram hashtags—#wellnessexpert, #wellnessinfluencer, #wellnesscoach, and #wellnessblogger—and see who pops up. Another great hack is to search the people you already follow and admire; people who *could* be your competitors. Head to their Instagram profile and hit the down-arrow button next to their email tab on their profiles. This will pop open the drop-down, "Suggestions for You," which is a left-to-right scrolling list of like-minded personal brands you most likely have never heard of before! This provides a rich database to begin your competitive research.

Say you're in technology. Instead of googling "technology CEOs," search "top tech CEOs of 2021." You want to look for lists such as media hits from outlets like *Fast Company*, *Forbes*, VentureBeat, Business Insider, CNBC, and beyond. Since these kinds of articles are subjective based on the media outlet, you will find a wide array of people, some of whom you might have heard of, and many you probably haven't. This is great! Seek out a series of these people and then begin to google their specific names. Hello, rabbit hole.

Caveat: feel free to use both Instagram and Google in your research, regardless of what industry you are in, to expand your findings. There are no hard and fast rules here.

I would recommend identifying at least five to ten competitors and then narrowing them down to your final three, based upon who resonates with you the most. You want a final list of people who are closest to your brand and stage in your business. Make sure they have a robust presence online. This means they are active on at least one to two social media channels, they create original content (via a blog, podcast, videos, events, speaking engagements, or books) and have garnered a decent amount of PR. Having a personal website is a big bonus.

Yet, don't forget to listen to your heart. I want you to choose people who you connect with on a personal level too. If you feel an emotional connection to their brand, it will enhance your creativity. To boot, if you feel connected to this person, your own audience most likely would as well.

Once you have determined your final three, it's time to get down to business and get tactical. As you observe their platforms, you might find that none of them have capitalized on YouTube or perhaps only one has a really strong visually branded website or maybe all three have national speaking careers, but no one is tapping niche markets. This is the white space! And there is much to be found there.

Let's find yours.

WHITE SPACE ANALYSIS

Below you will find three competitive analysis worksheets. Take the names of your three finalized competitors and write one name at the top of each sheet.

You are now going to look at the nuances, specific actions, and choices of your competitors and fill your worksheets out by conducting qualitative and quantitative analyses.

COMPETITOR NO. 1

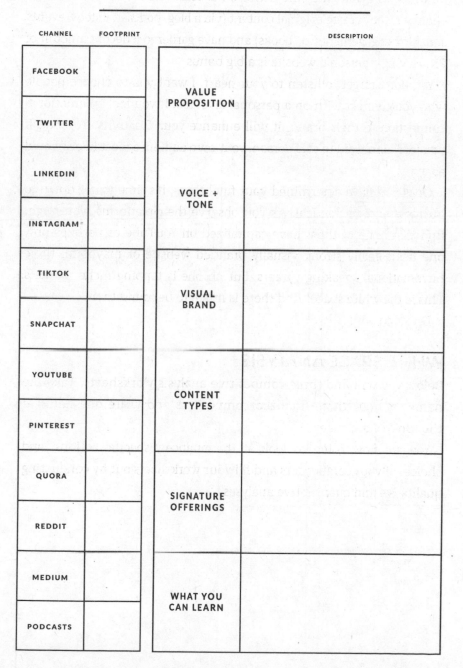

CHANNEL	FOOTPRINT		DESCRIPTION
FACEBOOK		VALUE PROPOSITION	
TWITTER			
LINKEDIN		VOICE + TONE	
INSTAGRAM			
TIKTOK		VISUAL BRAND	
SNAPCHAT			
YOUTUBE		CONTENT TYPES	
PINTEREST			
QUORA		SIGNATURE OFFERINGS	
REDDIT			
MEDIUM		WHAT YOU CAN LEARN	
PODCASTS			

COMPETITOR NO. 2

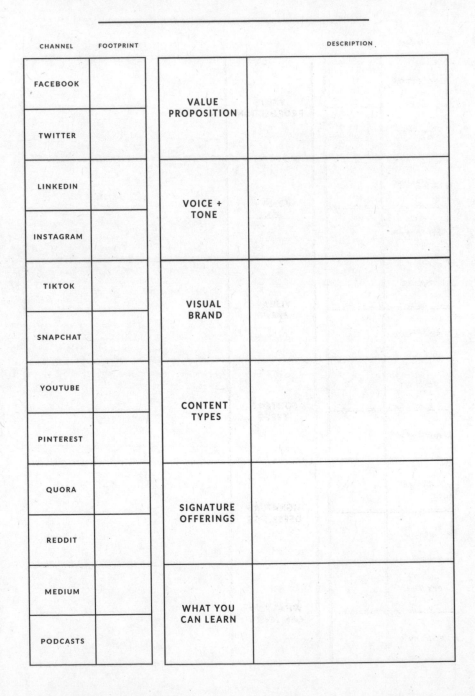

CHANNEL	FOOTPRINT		DESCRIPTION
FACEBOOK		VALUE PROPOSITION	
TWITTER			
LINKEDIN		VOICE + TONE	
INSTAGRAM			
TIKTOK		VISUAL BRAND	
SNAPCHAT			
YOUTUBE		CONTENT TYPES	
PINTEREST			
QUORA		SIGNATURE OFFERINGS	
REDDIT			
MEDIUM		WHAT YOU CAN LEARN	
PODCASTS			

COMPETITOR NO. 3

CHANNEL	FOOTPRINT
FACEBOOK	
TWITTER	
LINKEDIN	
INSTAGRAM	
TIKTOK	
SNAPCHAT	
YOUTUBE	
PINTEREST	
QUORA	
REDDIT	
MEDIUM	
PODCASTS	

	DESCRIPTION
VALUE PROPOSITION	
VOICE + TONE	
VISUAL BRAND	
CONTENT TYPES	
SIGNATURE OFFERINGS	
WHAT YOU CAN LEARN	

QUALITATIVE ANALYSIS

Let's explore the descriptive words, feelings, visuals, essence, offerings, and the overarching presence of your competitors. This is the more subjective part of the process; however, as you answer the questions in each category, do your best to monitor your own judgments, reactions, or insecurities that might come up. The goal is to simply observe.

- *Value proposition: In a few sentences, what does this person uniquely offer to the world?*
- *Voice + tone: Describe their brand personality in four to five keywords. Also pay attention to their use of capital letters, specific punctuation, emojis, or hashtags. This informs the voice and tone.*
- *Visual brand: What color palette, imagery, and photography do they use, and what does that tell you about their brand?*
- *Content types: What main sources of content do they use to market their brand? Is it a blog series, a podcast, or a video series? Are they actively using email marketing? Do they focus strictly on speaking? Do they have a book in the market?*
- *Signature offerings: What are their signature offerings, meaning what makes them money (e.g., coaching, speaking gigs, online courses, digital memberships, consulting, events, workshops, retreats, etc.)?*
- *What you can learn: If you had to narrow it down, what is the number one thing you can learn from this competitor?*

QUANTITATIVE ANALYSIS

In your quantitative analysis, you will look at the numbers of your competitors' digital footprint. For purposes of this research, I have included all possible channels and platforms at the top of your competitor analysis worksheets. If a competitor doesn't hold a presence on a particular channel, just write "NA," for not applicable. If they do have a presence, and you cannot find how many followers, visits, or downloads that particular channel has, take your best guess based upon the *surrounding data*.

Snapchat, for example, doesn't allow you to see how many followers a person has, unlike Instagram and Twitter. However, you can see some-one's Snapchat "score" (the combined number of snaps received and sent), which is the surrounding data. The higher the Snapchat score, the more safely you can assume that person has a high engagement and therefore is maximizing this channel.

It can also be tricky to find true data on podcast downloads, unless that podcast host or producer openly shares it, which is rare. If you can't find this information, then a great place to look for surrounding data is in the reviews. If a podcast show has 50 reviews versus say, 3,500, you can make a safe assumption that their podcast engagement is comparatively low.

For these less-specific data points, write "red" for a small presence, "yellow" for a mid-size presence, and "green" for a large presence. The rest of the quantitative data (i.e., social media following, etc.) will be easy to find. Use your instincts in this process while staying as objective as possible when it comes to the elusive data.

FIND YOUR WHITE SPACE

Taking your renewed mindset of the word *competition*, your qualitative and quantitative insights, and your newfound understanding of your unique light, it's time to find the white space. This is your final step toward refining your brand positioning with evermore razor sharp clarity before we dive into the development of your strategy. Pay attention to where you can shine, and what makes YOU different. Will it be writing, speaking, or podcasting? Perhaps it's a mix of all three. Which social media channels will you capitalize on that others are not? How will you differentiate your look and feel? What are the ownable qualities of your brand voice? That's where the rubber will really meet the road.

Remember: there is only one you. There is nothing more essential to your self-worth than owning that simple fact. By the same token, there is nothing more empowering, freeing, and heart-opening than rooting for other people. Blend your originality with your inspiration to get closer to your one-of-a-kind personal brand. Sure, it's all been said before. But no one has said it like you.

Be.

inspired

Don't judge or project your negative
perceptions onto your competition. At the
same time, don't allow yourself to feel
inferior or intimidated. Let your competitors
INSPIRE you by showing what's possible.
If they can do it, you can too.

CHAPTER 10

THOUGHT LEADERS THINK

"A vision without a strategy
remains an illusion."

Lee Bolman

In the early days of SimplyBe., I was working with a super tough client. Let's call him Sam. Sam was your quintessential serial entrepreneur, having built and sold multiple companies. He was cocky, impatient, reactionary, impulsive, and always "sooo busy." He made me shake with anxiety.

He had hired us to help build his platform, as he was embarking on fundraising from investors for his latest company and needed our help in positioning him as a thought leader in his industry. He was one of my very first clients, and I had a lot to prove. Not just to him but to myself. So we created a strategy that included a powerful blogging calendar that we would amplify through his personal website, Medium, and LinkedIn. We would use this blog content to power all of his microcontent across Instagram, Facebook, and his email marketing to cast a wide net and saturate his audience with his clear credibility and generate buzz. We came up with a slew of unique, engaging topics that ranged from his trading expertise to amplify his credibility, to his lessons learned from being a new dad to demonstrate his relatability.

At SimplyBe., we have a phenomenal ghostwriting team that works to develop all of our written content for our clients (blogs, video scripts, social media posts, and more). We set up "knowledge extraction" phone calls or sometimes have our clients send us lengthy emails or voice notes around a specific topic to accelerate all content development. We literally will extract their knowledge and turn it into polished, well-defined, written work in the client's voice, demonstrating the client's expertise. It's a true partnership.

The problem with Sam was that he wanted us to write his blogs entirely for him . . . without him. Getting him to take a phone call with us proved near impossible. Instead, he would text us a random idea and expect that to be enough. He believed that, as his team, we should be fully responsible for writing all of his content *as* him, for him, without him.

As you can probably guess, this did not go too well. Over time, it became incredibly frustrating for me and my team to do our jobs effectively, and we were unable to scale his platform because we had so little to work with. This resulted in Sam becoming equally frustrated with us, and his engagement ended. We have since updated our policies at SimplyBe. and have clearly defined client expectations. I have learned that no client retainer was worth the expense of my own self-worth. Over the years, this belief, along with a new set of boundaries, has allowed us to attract more and more of our right clients.

And yet, I was so grateful for Sam, as he was one of my biggest aha moments in running my business.

Sam wanted to be a "thought leader," but he didn't want to *think*.

Thought leaders are defined as such because they do just that—they think. They are leaders in new ways of thinking. They illuminate original ideas, perspectives, concepts, and visions that have yet to be considered, let alone discussed openly.

You don't need to be a PhD to be a thought leader. You are YOU, with your one-of-a-kind personal and professional history to disseminate. That's YOUR PhD, and it's enough to build your thought leadership. You just have to have the willingness, the courage, and the time to put pen to paper, fingers to keyboard, face to camera, or mouth to microphone and share your knowledge.

Yourself.

That's what true thought leaders do. And when they are ready to take it to the next level and need support in doing so, they enlist some help. (Or, they buy this book.)

Look at that . . . you're already ahead of the game.

Time to strategize.

WINNERS AND LOSERS

Riddle me this: Would you build a house without a blueprint? Would you move to a new city without researching it? Would you quit your job without some sort of plan?

You're a smart soul, so I am going to safely assume the answer would be hell no.

While it's essential (and awesome!) that you now know your brand message, have a slew of content topics at your fingertips, and have a deeper understanding of how and where you can stand out in the landscape, that is only half of the equation.

Your brand message is the art. Your strategy is the science.

Those who build (and follow) an actual strategy possess the defining factor between the winners and losers in the personal branding game.

Sorry not sorry.

Having a brand without a strategy is pointless. Without a strategy, you are without objectives (a.k.a. direction) and have nothing to measure against to see if you're succeeding. Without a strategy, growing your brand, and thus your business, is nearly impossible. Without a strategy, you're aimlessly lost in the sea of tactics with no sense of what to actually *do* on a daily, weekly, monthly, quarterly, or annual basis.

Sounds miserably overwhelming, doesn't it?

But *with* a strategy, you have a road map. An actual plan. A playbook on what to do and why. With a strategy, you identify your goals, define how you're going to get from point A to point Z, and (perhaps most excitingly) effectively maximize your time for the greatest impact. A strategy streamlines all the possibilities of what you *could* do to get your brand seen into what you *should* do to ensure that it does.

Having a strategy is one of the best case studies in the "slow down to speed up" philosophy. Investing the time in your strategy upfront will accelerate your business beyond your wildest imagination. Your marketing strategy powers your business, connecting you to your community, clients, potential employers, partners, audience, and the media. Your strategy enables them to discover your existence and build a connection and ultimately empowers them to invest their time, energy, and resources in you. And since your customers fuel the life source of your business, you can justifiably say that without a clear strategy, your business simply won't and can't survive. That's how critical a strategy is.

Without a rock solid strategy, you run the risk of suffering from what I call the Personal Brand Opportunity Loss.

You see, the people who win online *are* the people who win in business. They are winning not necessarily because they are better, more qualified, or even more experienced than you. The reason they are winning is because people simply know they *exist*. The losers aren't losers because they suck at their craft. They are losing because they are invisible.

Having a crystal clear brand message isn't enough. The world has to *know* your brand and understand your brand. You have to shout it from the rooftops.

Strategically, that is.

NO SNAP JUDGMENTS

Many people think that simply posting on Instagram five times a week at the same time every day is a strategy. Let's be clear about something: Social media is where you grow your community. It's a microphone and a conduit to amplify your core content. But it is not where a brand is born, or where it lives and dies. So, if you're on a mission to become an Instagram celebrity or a YouTube star, I hope you can tell by now that you're reading the wrong book.

Let's take a (brief) trip down the digital memory lane.

In 2008, at the dawn of the social media explosion, Facebook was all the rage, Twitter was too, and no one gave a shit about LinkedIn. In 2010 along came Instagram, and Facebook had to compete with the very channel it would acquire two years later. A few short years after that, Snapchat burst on the scene with its brand-new, real-time video features. Faster than you could add a face filter, Instagram Stories launched with the exact same features, only with a bigger audience. And just like that, Snapchat's market share (and valuation) decreased.

As I'm writing this book, everyone is talking about TikTok giving Instagram a run for its money. Meanwhile, it's harder to grow on Twitter than ever before, and LinkedIn is slowly becoming the next best place to be. And let's not forget about the power of Pinterest, the depth of YouTube, and—does anybody remember Periscope? All this change is in just the past decade alone! Who knows what tomorrow will bring? I'm dizzy just thinking about it.

Social media is fast and fleeting. Your personal brand is not. And you're playing the long game, remember?

If you want your personal brand to stand the test of time, then you have to build your brand—and thus your strategy—beyond social media.

As you know by now, an authentic personal brand message has the ability to elevate you as a thought leader, and thought leaders are in the business of creating *original* ideas by way of sharing *original* content. And original content comes in many forms: blogs, videos, podcasts, books, workshops, online courses, webinars, retreats, trainings, coaching programs, consulting, speaking, and beyond. We call this your "Pinnacle Content." More on that in just a moment.

In order to grow a tribe, open doors to speak, get paid more money for your time and services, and create a fucking movement, you must dream up and present original ideas into the world and do so consistently. This is what will position you as the expert in your space.

And you do this through creating original content to power your marketing strategy, not your social media strategy. That's the distinction between thought leaders and social media influencers.

Which one would you rather be?

Thought leaders think.
That's why they are called thought leaders.

CHAPTER 11

INTRODUCING THE PINNACLE CONTENT FRAMEWORK

"Simplicity is the ultimate form of sophistication."

Leonardo da Vinci

Before I launched SimplyBe., I half launched it.

I had just quit my corporate job and quite literally walked away from a six-figure salary (plus benefits, bonus, and a corporate card) with nothing in savings. Needless to say, I was scared shitless.

As a safety net, I decided to team up with another ad agency for some security. At first, working with them I felt not only safe but validated. They wanted my personal branding expertise, and I was eager to learn from their process. After a few months, we decided to construct a formal deal: they would license the brand SimplyBe. and put me on a super modest salary. We would hunt for business together, and I would get a small percentage commission of the net profits. The final caveat of the deal was that my title would no longer be CEO as I had originally positioned myself (since it was, after all, my company), but rather General Manager of the SimplyBe. Division. I remember the founder of the agency telling me at one point that I was not equipped to run a company, and that I didn't understand the ins and outs of business. "That's what we'll do," he said proudly and convincingly. "You, Jess, are meant to be the face." I believed him. Inside, my intuition was screaming at me.

One morning, a few of us were sitting in the conference room, working on a strategy for a new client. We had been there for over three hours, talking in circles. The white board, which took up the entire wall because it *was* the wall, was completely covered with unending bullet points, graphs, pie charts, metaphoric imagery, and illegible notes scribbled in a mix of different people's handwriting. I felt woozy just looking at it.

As the morning-long strategy session was wrapping for lunch, I had no idea what the game plan was. Shit, I didn't even understand what the *aim* was. I don't think any of us did. I thought to myself, "There has to be a simpler way to do this."

The word *strategy* evokes the notion of complexity. At least it used to for me. It's fair to say that a lot of agencies believe that the more detailed, elaborate, time intensive, and radical a strategy is, the more creative they can call themselves. I call bullshit. I believe the simpler a strategy is, the more effective it becomes. At the end of the day, a strategy that's set up to succeed should take the path of least resistance. The more overwhelming your brand strategy feels, the more overwhelmed your audience, consumers, and clients will feel too.

The not-so-surprising moral of this story is that I backed out of that crappy deal. I finally listened to my intuition and called bullshit on that founder who convinced me I couldn't build a company on my own. I realized that I didn't need anyone to validate me. I could validate myself. And I did.

I also validated a new way to build a strategy, and wouldn't you know . . . *it's really fucking simple.*

INTRODUCING THE PINNACLE CONTENT FRAMEWORK

It's not just agencies who overcomplicate strategies. People do too. It's likely that when you hear the word *strategy*, you, too, envision fancy

THE PINNACLE CONTENT FRAMEWORK™

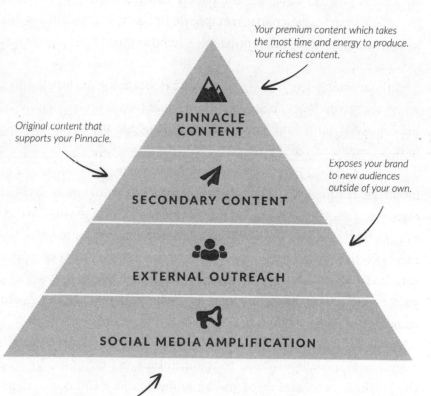

Your premium content which takes the most time and energy to produce. Your richest content.

Original content that supports your Pinnacle.

PINNACLE CONTENT

Exposes your brand to new audiences outside of your own.

SECONDARY CONTENT

EXTERNAL OUTREACH

SOCIAL MEDIA AMPLIFICATION

Amplifies your brand message and content daily.

color-coded spreadsheets, messy white boards, twelve-month granular time lines with 10-point font and, heaven forbid, an appendix.

Gag!

It's time to set the record straight: building a strategy is simple. I firmly believe that people avoid building their brand platforms and really doing the work of showing up for the world in fully authentic form for one reason and one reason only: overwhelm. Are you really going to let the assumption that something is challenging prevent you from living out your dreams?

I am here to tell you that building a strategy can (and should) be the furthest thing from overwhelming. Remember, building your brand isn't about making a ton of noise. It's about making the *right* noise to the *right* audience. It should possess a clear path toward your goal. An easy-to-follow line that gets you from point A to point Z. It should be inspired not by the minutiae but by its target.

It should be defined by the pinnacle of your success.

Enter the trademarked SimplyBe.'s Pinnacle Content Framework. Now that you understand your brand identity by way of the Hologram, your brand content through the Supernova, and your white space through your competitive analysis, the Pinnacle Content Framework lays the rock-solid foundation for your brand strategy. And no good thought leader worth her five-figure speaking fee is without one.

Whether your objective is to grow your mailing list, sell your online course to more people, get asked to speak more often, increase your consulting fees, or yes, even grow your Instagram following, the Pinnacle Content Framework is a universal tool that will easily allow you to put a method to the marketing madness to grow your business.

Let's take this beauty and break it down piece by piece.

Your Pinnacle Content: The Peak of Your Brand

According to the dictionary, the word *pinnacle* is defined as follows:

- *The most successful point: the culmination*
- *A high-pointed piece of rock*

Your premium content which takes the most time and energy to produce. Your richest content.

PINNACLE CONTENT

At SimplyBe., we define *pinnacle* in the following ways:

- *That which validates the most successful point(s) in your career*
- *The culmination of all your hard work and experience into your expert point of view*
- *The most critical component of your strategy*

Why is it critical? Without Pinnacle Content to share online, you won't come across as a thought leader. Pinnacle Content insinuates that you invest time, energy, and, potentially, resources into serving your audience and thereby demonstrates that you care about them. Most of all, it elevates you as the expert in your industry. Without Pinnacle Content, the best-case scenario is that you'll come across as a social media influencer. Worst case, you won't come across at all, because no one will know that you exist, let alone what you stand for.

So what exactly does Pinnacle Content look like, and more importantly, what does it look like for *you*?

When we hear the word *content*, we are keen to think of the written word and anything in the literary world. But today, content comes to life in the digital realm, in physical form, in experiences, and in intimate conversations.

In other words: *everything* is content.

Let's examine the following key rules about Pinnacle Content that would be helpful to keep in mind when developing your own:

- *It's the most valuable information to your audience.*
- *It takes the most time and effort to create.*
- *It can be a "marathon" (something you do all year long, like a weekly blog) or a "sprint" (something you do for a concentrated period, like a mastermind event).*
- *It's consistent, meaning it happens weekly, monthly, quarterly, biannually, or annually.*

When it comes to choosing your own Pinnacle Content, I like to say that there are four ways we can "talk to the world" today:

1. **In-person events**
2. **Written content**
3. **Video content**
4. **Audio content**

If that's not enough to get your juices flowing, let's dive deeper into what these four content avenues could look like with some variation inspiration:

- *Variations of events: Workshops, networking events, retreats, masterminds, panels, conferences, summits, webinars, livestreams, Zoom events, etc.*

- **Variations of writing:** *Long-form and short-form blogging, list articles and written interviews, premium content (e-books, white papers, tip sheets), formally published work, and so on.*
- **Variations of video:** *Video series, web shows, live casts, Insta Stories, Snapchat campaigns, TikTok videos, webinars, Zoomcasts, video seminars, YouTube channels, IGTV, and so on.*
- **Sharing value through audio:** *Podcasts are all the rage now, with well over a million options in Apple Podcasts now, ranging across thousands of industries, and you can also broadcast audio content through Stitcher, Libsyn, PodBean, Spotify, Transistor, Buzzsprout, SoundCloud, Captivate, and so on. Lest we forget, there are other variations of audio, such as meditations, songs, and audio files to complement blogs, courses, and online memberships. We are at the tip of the iceberg when it comes to the power of audio content.*

When selecting your Pinnacle Content, it's important to play to your strengths and decide to create something you actually enjoy creating. Because if you don't enjoy it, you won't do it. At the same time, it has to be strategic. Ask yourself the following questions to choose Pinnacle Content that makes the most sense for you and your brand:

- *Who is my target client?*
- *Where do they spend most of their time?*
- *What kind of content will resonate with them?*
- *What do I like to create?*
- *Why?*
- *What resources do I have (time, money, a team)?*

Pinnacle Content doesn't just provide you with the opportunity to share your expertise. It also elevates the perception people have of you. This isn't a popularity contest. This is the power of perception. Perception is branding. You hold the power to create your own perception with your Pinnacle Content.

The 80/20 Rule: The Rest of Your Pinnacle Content Framework

There's an age-old adage that states: "20 percent of your effort should account for 80 percent of your results." The same rule applies for your content strategy.

Your Pinnacle Content is your 20 percent. It's where you will put most of your time, effort, and energy. It's the macro that will accelerate the other 80 percent of your strategy, or the micro. Meaning, you have already done the heavy lifting by creating your Pinnacle Content. The rest of your Pinnacle Content Framework is then powered by taking your Pinnacle Content and breaking it into little pieces and spreading it across various media and platforms.

Some people love to read blogs, while others prefer video. Some adore social media, while others cherish their newsletter subscriptions. Still others prefer to listen to an expert in the comfort of their own home via a podcast versus attending an event to listen to one live. Remember: this is about knowing your audience as much as it is about understanding your own content creation preferences. Regardless of your medium preference, the goal is the same: to get your brand seen as much as possible.

Secondary Content: This Ain't the Field of Dreams

Let's now look at the next component of the Pinnacle Content Framework, your Secondary Content channel strategy. Why do you need Secondary Content? For starters, your personal brand strategy isn't the field of dreams. You can't just build your Pinnacle Content and expect people to show up drooling in droves. You cannot just launch your podcast, publish your blog, launch your web show, or host your event and expect your community to know it's there without a dedicated promotion around it.

Think of your Secondary Content as your 1:1 effort in promoting your Pinnacle Content, meaning that the only "job" of your Secondary Content is to send people directly and solely to your Pinnacle Content. In a perfect world, Secondary Content takes less time to create than Pinnacle.

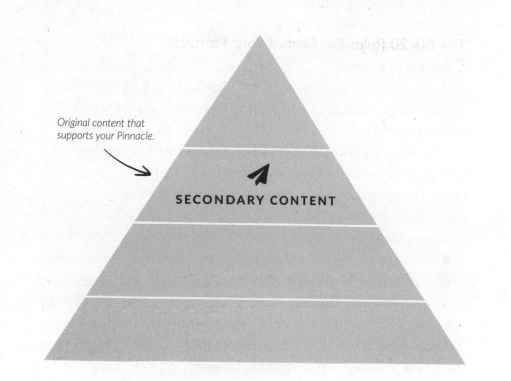

Original content that supports your Pinnacle.

SECONDARY CONTENT

Here are some powerful examples of Secondary Content in action, using the Pinnacle Content variation inspiration list from earlier.

PINNACLE CONTENT	SECONDARY CONTENT CHANNEL
A three-minute video you share on LinkedIn on the five key insights on your industry's latest trends	A 500-word microblog highlighting three out of the five key insights in the video, with a call to action and hyperlink to watch the final two in the video
A forty-five-minute podcast episode interviewing a fellow expert in your space	Comprehensive show notes you publish in a blog on your website, inclusive of powerful quotes by your guest

PINNACLE CONTENT	SECONDARY CONTENT CHANNEL
A 1,500-word blog you publish on your website about the best places to travel in style on a budget	A dedicated newsletter sent to your email list, inclusive of the opening paragraph to the blog, with a call to action to "read more" and a hyperlink to the URL of the blog
An annual conference you're producing for 300 people in Costa Rica	A three-part video series with details on (1) the conference's content, (2) the gorgeous locale, and (3) previous attendee testimonials on the event itself, with a call to action to buy tickets to the event
An online course you're selling for $500 to your community	A free quiz + report they can take to find out what they need to do to prepare for the course, incentivizing them to purchase while capturing dedicated email addresses to your list
A private workshop training for thirty people	A three-minute scripted promotion and explanation of your workshop at the top of every podcast episode, with a clear call to action to register on your website

The possibilities are limitless. Just remember that all Secondary Content should do the following:

- *Directly amplify your Pinnacle Content*
- *Take less time to create than your Pinnacle Content*
- *Be your largest effort in promoting your Pinnacle Content*

External Outreach: The Key to the Lockbox

Derek Halpern, founder of Social Triggers, is one of my all-time favorite digital marketing experts. Not only have I followed Derek's work for years but I had the great fortune of working with him one-on-one in the only mastermind he's ever hosted. Since then, he's become my unofficial on-call marketing guru, and I turn to him whenever I am in desperate need of direction.

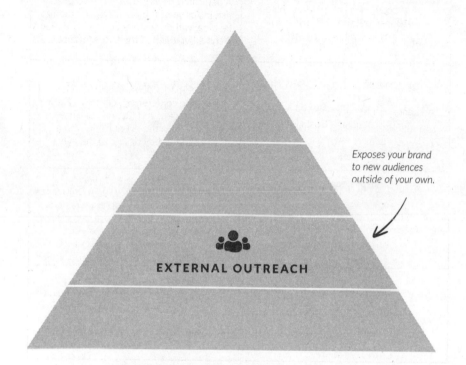

Exposes your brand to new audiences outside of your own.

EXTERNAL OUTREACH

Derek taught me a brilliantly simple concept: "on-site events" versus "off-site events." Your on-site events are activities that take place on your own platform and your own channels. On-site events help you to create affinity, deepen relationships, and cultivate awareness within your own, already established audience.

Off-site events, on the flip side, are an effort to get your brand in front of audiences besides your own to create exposure and ultimately add these new audiences to yours so you can grow. Find enough off-site event opportunities, and your brand awareness begins to grow beyond what you could ever possibly produce on your own. This is an incredibly potent part of your strategy.

Off-site events come in various forms. At SimplyBe., we call this part of your Pinnacle Content Framework "External Outreach." This essentially leverages your Pinnacle Content to showcase your expertise and credibility in order to open up doors to get featured on outside channels. Your Pinnacle Content is the key that unlocks newfound notoriety.

This is a spin on traditional PR. I believe that personal brands, over product brands, have a unique ability to innovatively reach new audiences, share their expertise, and thus grow their brands far beyond what the traditional media hit can do.

Here are some great examples of External Outreach:

- *Digital publications: digital news and entertainment websites, video interviews, and blog features*
- *Social media partnerships: Instagram takeovers, IGTV interviews, co-hosted Instagram Lives, Snapchat interviews, brand partnerships, and special features*
- *Events: panels, fireside chats, keynotes, emceeing occasions, and networking opportunities*
- *Traditional media: TV segments, radio interviews, and print publication features*
- *Collaborations with people inside and out of your industry through content, events, and experiences*
- *Podcast interviews*
- *Awards submissions*

We will be diving deep into External Outreach in the next chapter. But for now, take a look at the list above and start to zero in on what approach to External Outreach feels the most aligned to your brand goals, and what feels the most comfortable or natural for you to partake in. From there, we will chart the course to External Outreach strategy.

Social Media Amplification: Your Megaphone

Isn't it interesting that social media is the very *last* place we end up? Most people think social media is the holy grail of personal branding.

It's okay if you shared this misconception too. With the recent boom of social media (and everyone's obsession with it), it's an easy mistake to make. Let the record show that social media is a place for tactics. It's not your strategy.

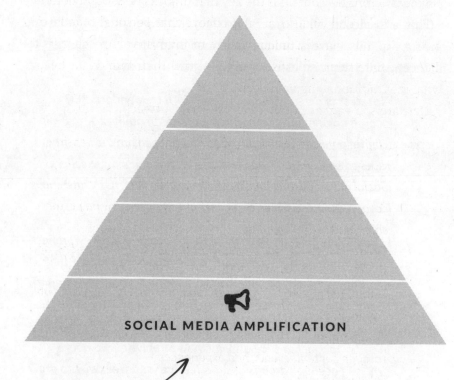

Amplifies your brand message and content daily.

I am not undervaluing the dynamism and effectiveness of social media. Quite the opposite. To be frank, SimplyBe.'s Pinnacle Content Framework method cannot—and will not—succeed without a strong emphasis on social media.

That said, I also don't believe anyone needs to be focused (let alone present) on every single channel. Not only because your time (and your sanity) is your most sacred commodity but also because it's just not strategic. The overarching evolution of social media has brought us many channels to choose from, and they now all serve different purposes, for different types of brands, with different types of audiences. I recommend choosing one channel minimum, two maximum, to focus on. The key is to go narrow and deep versus shallow and wide.

In order to decide what channel (or two) might be the most strategic one for you, let's explore the purpose of each of the main channels today, along with what industries work best within them.

- *Pinterest is a digital "mood board" with tremendous SEO (search engine optimization) power and an ability to "tag" pins that help you rank high in the Pinterest feed, and it is a great place to source traffic to your own website. It's an excellent platform for lifestyle industries like home, art, travel, fashion, beauty, design, and food.*

- *Facebook is industry agnostic and a place to create awareness through brand pages. Facebook has evolved into one of the most powerful online advertising platforms today, with unparalleled targeting abilities. This therefore makes it the hardest place to grow at scale organically, and you must "pay to play" in order to reach a wide audience. At SimplyBe., we adore private Facebook groups as an effective (and free) way to grow niche communities.*

- *LinkedIn is ideal for business professionals, executives, entrepreneurs, within B2B industries. Today, it is the number one place to create thought leadership through an optimized page and by distributing original content via blogs, livestreams, videos, and feed posts.*

- *Twitter is an ideal channel for politics, sports, media, celebrity, entrepreneurship, venture capital, and technology. It's more of a listening tool than a posting tool and a great place to stay on top of daily trends.*

- *Instagram* is another great platform for lifestyle businesses, but with one billion users, there's a niche for everyone. It is the number one place to create community through its unparalleled versatility of features: the grid (for visual storytelling), Stories (for a behind-the-scenes look), livestreams (for real-time connection to your audience), IGTV (long-form video for deeper brand affinity), and Reels, 15 second multi-clip videos to keep your audience even more engaged.

- *Snapchat* is ideal for personal brands looking to target the younger millennial base, as well as Gen Z. Its focus is on 1:1 messaging and relationship building through its Stories versus holistic brand storytelling. Its power is found in its humor and the sheer fun of its user experience.

- *YouTube* is less of a social media channel and more of a search engine. (It's owned by Google, making it the second largest search engine available.) It's industry agnostic as well. "How to" tutorials perform beautifully here. If you're keen on video, it's a great place to invest time and resources if a top objective is to drive massive traffic to your website.

- *TikTok:* The latest social media addiction, er, application to emerge is this video-sharing social channel that lets anyone become a lip-syncing sensation or dance-competition household hero. It's currently all the rage for Gen Z, but more and more users are starting to jump on the TikTok train, close to a billion in fact. Whether dancing it out to Lil Uzi Vert is your thing or not, there is one thing to note about TikTok: it's a pop-culture zeitgeist, making it an amazing place to keep your finger on the pulse of what's trending.

With your laser-sharp, value-based brand message informing your thoughtful, strategic Pinnacle Content, you now know exactly *what* to disseminate into that megaphone of yours on a daily basis via social media.

PUTTING IT ALL TOGETHER: MY PINNACLE CONTENT FRAMEWORK IN ACTION

Ta-da! Here it is. Let's dive in, or should I say . . . *climb up*?

Sitting at the top is the SimplyBe. Podcast, my main vehicle for connecting with my target audience and what I use to teach them how to build their brands and live their best life. Many of the concepts I write about in this book started as episodes on my podcast! That's because my Pinnacle Content is where I do what I do best: inspire my audience to build a brilliant brand and a kick-ass life by creating a stronger connection to their authentic truths.

Second(ary) is my newsletter. Email marketing is a powerful tool that anyone can use to build an ownable audience. Since I know Mark Zuckerberg owns my social media following, I focused on my email list. My mailing list belongs to me, and since people hold their email addresses and inboxes sacred these days, I know my mailing list consists of my most loyal and adoring fans of my brand. Like clockwork, I send a newsletter to them each week on the day my podcast drops to drive additional eyes—or, I should say, ears—to my show. I also include links to the latest blogs, articles, or videos I'm consuming to add even more value to my audience. Starting to see a pattern, right?

Moving right along, for External Outreach, I focus on getting hits in digital publications, getting booked to speak at events, and racking up industry awards, all in the name of getting my message from my original content (hello, podcast!) to reach audiences outside of my own. This piece of the Pinnacle Content Framework is all about boosting your credibility. For me, it's about attracting more of the right clients to my business—which are probably the people reading pubs like *Inc.* and *Forbes*.

Finally, social media. You'll see that even though I ardently believe in the power of social media as a tool to amplify your brand, I'm not on *every* channel. Far from it. Based on where my audience is hanging out online, I've chosen to focus solely on Instagram and LinkedIn. By narrowing it down to a couple of platforms, I'm able to be really strategic

JESSICA'S PINNACLE CONTENT FRAMEWORK™

Solo and interview style show dropping weekly on Apple Podcasts, Spotify, Stitcher, and company website.

Weekly newsletter offering free value, directing listeners to the podcast and promoting SimplyBe. products, events, and offerings.

THE SIMPLYBE. PODCAST

Reaching new audiences via digital press opportunities and speaking engagements.

EMAIL MARKETING

EXTERNAL OUTREACH

SOCIAL MEDIA AMPLIFICATION: INSTAGRAM & LINKEDIN

Original content designed to target clientele and to provide and foster community.

with my content on these channels. For example, I post audiograms on Instagram to tease my podcast. And I share my latest press hit—and SimplyBe.'s latest products—on LinkedIn. We'll go deep on how to truly maximize social media to work for you a little later on.

So guess what? That's it! Holy shit, that was easy, right?! A strategy doesn't have to be complicated. It just has to be smart.

One caveat before we move on: This is what my Pinnacle Content Framework looked like at the time I was writing this book. But the year before, it looked quite a bit different, and I can imagine, as you're reading this now, it's evolved once again (ahem, you may or may not be reading my Pinnacle Content right this second).

Like any good strategy, your content strategy, a.k.a. your Pinnacle Content—might change with time—and that's okay. That's because *you* change with time. In fact, that's exactly how you make it work.

YOUR PINNACLE CONTENT FRAMEWORK

Alright, my friend. Time to put on your strategic thinking cap and get out your pencil. Using the worksheet below, create your own Pinnacle Content Framework. Consider your Personal Brand Hologram, use your Supernova for inspiration for specific content topics, and reexamine your competitive landscape. Then pulse check which Pinnacle Content feels the best for you based on your audience, your goals, and your own personal preferences and ensure that your Secondary Channel accelerates your work rather than adding to it. Identify which External Outreach strategies make the most sense for your business, and when it comes to social media, choose one or two channels to go deep on to mitigate your overwhelm.

The Pinnacle Content Framework is your own summit to climb. Follow your heart, trust your gut, and don't compare yourself to anyone else.

I believe in you.

And as soon as you believe in yourself, the game changes.

It's time to play.

YOUR PINNACLE CONTENT FRAMEWORK™

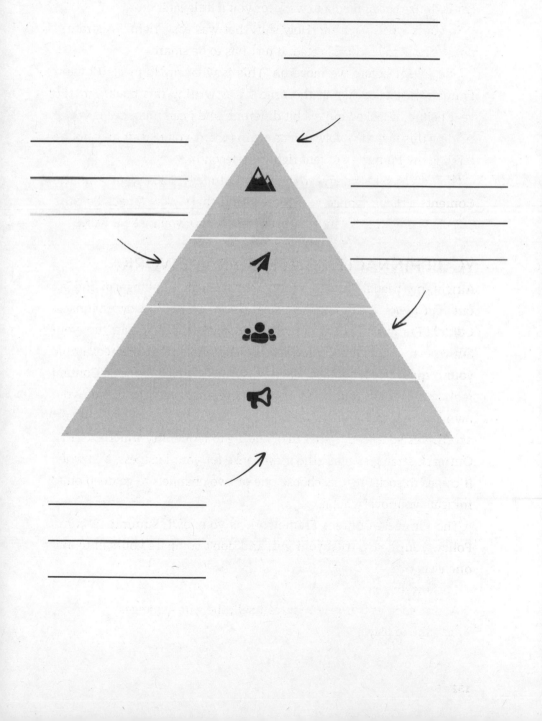

Be.
strategic

In the space between your vision
and your reality lives your strategy.

CHAPTER 12

SHOOT FOR THE STARS

"People do not buy goods or services.
People buy relations, stories, magic."

Seth Godin

Flash back to 2008. I had just launched my new, online women's lifestyle magazine, CheekyChicago.com. You might recall that prior to Cheeky, I had been a struggling actress/cocktail waitress. (Read: I knew absolutely nothing about running a magazine, let alone running a business.) To build buzz for the forthcoming debut of our website, I printed thousands of postcards that said, "CheekyChicago.com— Arriving Fashionably Late in October 2008." (Rather cheeky, eh?)

In true guerrilla-marketing-style form, I walked down every street in every neighborhood in Chicago passing out these postcards. I would walk shamelessly into nail salons, boutiques, restaurants, bars, coffee shops, tanning studios, you name it. I would politely request that the respective owner or manager put our postcards on their front desks, in their shopping bags, or on their bulletin boards. Surprisingly, a lot of them said yes. I did this for an entire summer leading up to our launch. On the day of the website's October debut, I hosted a launch party at a local bar, thinking that only my best friends and family would show.

Instead, three hundred people turned up. And ten thousand people went to the website that same day.

The next day, I woke up to find in my inbox my very first pitch from a publicist.

I was confused.

What exactly was I supposed to *do* with this? How did this person get my email? Was I supposed to . . . *respond*? What should I *say*?

You could call my introduction to the world of PR a rude awakening. Clearly I was green as fresh-cut grass, not even realizing that by way of launching a magazine I had become relevant to the media, and had become "the media" too, practically overnight.

Yet, I believe that one of my biggest assets at the dawn of my entrepreneurial career was my naiveté.

You see, I had no choice but to respond to these perfectly polished emails from strangers in my inbox and start to ask questions. Over time, my relationships with these people (who were technically called publicists and worked at PR firms) started to form. By way of these communications, I would end up featuring their clients in my magazine. More emails would come. To boot, I started making coffee dates with these newfound contacts. More emails came. Eventually I started getting invited to every restaurant, hotel, or fashion boutique opening, and I would receive packages of swag in the mail on the regular.

Naturally, I learned to LOVE the world of PR. Not because of the awesome parties and free shit. (Although that didn't hurt.) But because the PR world accelerated my job as a media professional. For those seven years running Cheeky, it was my literal job to know about "the next best thing" in Chicago. And each week, I had (literally) hundreds of those formerly "unexpected" emails in my inbox, filled with amazing new story ideas to choose from.

It was during this early time in my career that I learned the undeniable importance of PR. When a business, product, or person is featured in the media, it creates not only massive exposure but legitimacy and credibility. Being a member of the media myself, I too held a certain power. I knew that if I wrote a raving review of the newest restaurant opening—let's say Jane's Diner—the chances of thousands of women knowing about it overnight was a guarantee. Not to mention, the chances were high that a large percentage of those women would become actual patrons of Jane's Diner, ultimately impacting Jane's most important priority: revenue. This made PR features for these new "hot spots" essential to their success.

At least, at first.

During this chapter of my life, I learned that PR is a short game. It's about building buzz. It's about generating a lot of awareness within a concentrated period. It's an extremely effective and necessary strategy when you're launching something new or have something truly noteworthy or newsworthy to share.

But I couldn't write about Jane's Diner every week. Once was enough, and it was only relevant to my audience upon its opening. But I could write about a different restaurant each week. And instead of the restaurants themselves becoming the "thing" to know, *I* became the "person" to know. I, not the restaurants, had the influence.

I had no idea what I had accidentally done over the previous seven years running Cheeky. When I departed, I made the announcement via a single email to my network and a Facebook post. Within a week I had a whole book of business and a wait list. It wasn't the buzz I had built for products and places that I had been promoting all those years that created this response. It was the credibility that I had built in myself along the way that did it.

There's no denying the power of publicity. But personal branding is a different beast. As I said, in the world of PR, it's about building buzz. In the world of personal branding, it's about building a platform.

Flash forward to today. At SimplyBe., we take this exact approach with our clients, blending the power of a personal brand with the necessity of traditional PR. As a result, they don't just get featured by the media; they become the media.

It's time for you to do the same.

THE PR LANDSCAPE TODAY

A lot has changed since 2008.

And a lot has not.

Let's first give traditional PR the credit it deserves. Without a doubt, it increases brand credibility, while increasing the potential for more profits, sales, and leads. It undoubtedly changes the way people think about you and thereby enhances your online presence and professional perception.

I'll use myself as an example and my own experience in garnering traditional PR exposure. Upon launching SimplyBe., I was listed as the "Top Digital Marketer to Watch" in an article on *Inc.* and was featured in *Forbes* as a personal branding expert. Yes, this was undoubtedly a fantastic thing to be able to share in real time with my community (remember, my on-site event) and at the same to get seen by thousands of new potential readers on those two media platforms (off-site events).

But what has been proven to be the most compelling aspect of these respective media hits has been their longevity. Meaning, I am now forever able to say that I was listed on *Inc.* and *Forbes* as an expert in my field. That "stamp of approval" has opened up doors for me and my business beyond my wildest expectations. This is the true power of traditional PR.

But the landscape is shifting. With the introduction of not only blogging and social media, but publications *like Inc.*, *Forbes*, HuffPost, and Mashable anyone can hold the pen. Anyone can become an influencer, a contributor, or a journalist, if they choose to be. You see, those two features from *Inc.* and *Forbes* were written by aspiring thought leaders themselves. People who had worked really hard to become contributors to these hugely respected platforms, thereby increasing their own clout and thus, personal brands.

Traditional PR is evolving, and today, there is a vast array of new opportunities to build your own thought leadership. It doesn't have to stop and end with traditional PR. There are in fact many other opportunities to get seen outside your own platform in "nichier" places than Tier 1 media like

Forbes, *Fortune*, ABC, and NBC. Most of the time, reaching niche communities is the best way to move the needle in your business. This leads us to your External Outreach strategy, SimplyBe.'s evolution on traditional PR, and the third component of your Pinnacle Content Framework.

As you build your External Outreach strategy, I encourage you to think outside the box and to take advantage of the PR landscape today.

Now more than ever, you have the power to become *your own* media channel. I mean, this wasn't possible fifteen years ago. How fucking COOL is that?

I've said it before and I'll say it again: what an exciting time to be alive.

STAYING GROUNDED

Let's have a quick heart-to-heart.

When it comes to building your External Outreach strategy, patience is a virtue, my friend. So is realism.

Years ago, I was working with a client who *desperately* wanted "off-site" exposure. Let's call her Tina. Tina was a corporate consultant and had come to my agency to define her brand message and build her platform in order to become known as a leading voice in her industry. Through our discovery process, we learned that her number one objective was to get onto the TEDx stage. Now, it's my responsibility to ensure that we are building strategies for our clients that can achieve their goals. When we took a look at Tina's experience we found that she had never spoken on a single stage. At first, I didn't believe this was much of a detriment. After all, she was a really well-spoken, confident woman with a great message and to be frank, had a brilliant concept for her TEDx talk. We could easily build the path (and the platform) to get her there in time.

But when Tina explained that her expectation was for us to secure her that TEDx talk within three months, I was a bit baffled. I had to level with her. We could absolutely chart the course toward a TEDx talk, but I recommended we get her speaking on smaller and midscale stages in the short term in order to build her speaker reel. If she wanted to achieve something as competitive as speaking on a TEDx stage, it was essential to *demonstrate* that she was a sought-after thought leader, versus simply *declaring* it.

As you go forth in building your External Outreach strategy, it's important you stay grounded. Namely, on planet Earth.

At least for now.

Be.
seen

The ability to build authority by way
of PR opportunities is undeniable.
The opportunity to raise your pricing
and increase your net worth by
way of PR is unparalleled.

CHAPTER 13

INTRODUCING ORION'S ROADMAP

> "The cosmos is within us. We are made of star-stuff. We are the way for the Universe to know itself."
>
> *Carl Sagan*

In college, I took Astronomy 101 as an elective. For finals, I had to write a paper on the history of a constellation of my choice. This was precisely the same time I was avidly listening to Ani DiFranco while simultaneously breaking up with the first boy I ever loved. My favorite song at the time was "Untouchable Face." In it, there's a lyric Ani longingly sings, "I see Orion, and say nothing."

Naturally, I wrote my final paper on Orion, which means "the light of heaven." He was a controversial character described as a warrior who passionately chased love, challenged authority, sought transformation, and played by his own rules.

Needless to say, I broke up with the boy and peeled back on my Ani obsession. But my love for Orion still stands. To this day, whenever I look up and see him shining in the night sky, I take it as a sign that I am following my own destiny.

You are undoubtedly following yours. As you shoot for the stars, I encourage you to dream big. If you want to be on the cover of a magazine or a TED stage, fucking go for it. The only person holding you back from that possibility is you.

I am simply recommending that in the process of "going for it" you pace yourself. Setting realistic expectations, and building a tactical plan to achieve your dreams, is an essential part of your success—and peace of mind.

I have named this plan Orion's Roadmap. You are entitled to unabashedly, unapologetically shoot for the stars. And so with this road map, I want you to identify a dream hit. Say, TED or the cover of *Forbes* or a segment on the *Today Show*. Most people on the personal branding journey do not start out with a feature like that. You have to build your repertoire with a series of good-to-great "hits" that build a bigger story and more credible profile over time.

So, let's start by identifying your Orion's Star using the worksheet on the next page.

Now that you've identified your Orion's Star let's work backward toward your dream goal with Orion's Roadmap.

Starting at the bottom of the road map and working our way up, let's look at Tier 3, which consists of your Planets. Why? Because you're standing on one, friend. A Planet "hit" is a placement with local publications, talks on community panels, speaking for networking groups, and building off of personal relationships that are attainable. A Planet hit is one you could secure within the next three months, simply by tapping your connections or leveraging your mutual ones. In traditional PR terms (because we are still in the space of it), Planets reach boutique, niche audiences of fifty thousand to five hundred thousand unique monthly visitors (UMVs) or fewer.

Tier 2 is made up of your Moons. Why? Because, while you're not currently standing on the moon, you can see the moon from where you are today. The Moons allow you to get closer to Orion's Star, by establishing credibility and demonstrating experience. These are midsize publications,

IDENTIFYING YOUR ORION'S STAR

What is your dream feature?	
How would it impact your career?	
Does this feature align with your personal brand goals?	
How can you use your Pinnacle Content to get you there?	
Realistically, how long will it take to get there?	

ORION'S ROADMAP™

ORION'S STAR

MOONS

○ ○ ○ ○ ○

PLANETS

regional conferences, and panels, which are a bit more elusive and require a longer lead time. This is a hit you could secure within six months, by leveraging your Planets as you build your platform. Moons reach broader audiences of five hundred thousand to three million UMVs.

Tier 1, as you know by now, is Orion's Star. Why? Because you can't necessarily see Orion's Star from where you stand today. But as you ascend up into the personal branding stratosphere, collecting Planets and Moons, all while building your own audience through an expert platform with crystalized Pinnacle Content, your Orion's Star comes into focus. That pie-in-the-sky media hit is no longer so pie-in-the-sky. It's real. It's yours. Give yourself twelve plus months to get there, knowing that when you do, you have the potential to reach three million plus UMVs in a single shot. It's always worth the wait.

Let's take a look at my Orion's Roadmap as an example.

My dream is to be on the *Today Show* as a personal branding expert. I believe that if we don't claim what we want for our lives, how will the Universe ever know it needs to help us manifest it?

I quit playing small years ago. And I have not let the fact that I haven't reached certain stars deter me from knowing I am on the right path. Who knows . . . maybe I'll have been on *Today* by the time this book comes out. Maybe I won't have been. My job is to simply stay focused on blazing my path upward.

Throughout my entire career, I never underestimated the power of my Planets: niche publications and local outlets like *The Jam*, a live morning show in Chicago on WCIU, or *Lux & Concord*, a niche online magazine for women entrepreneurs. I collected a plethora of media hits at this planetary level before I felt confident pitching myself to my Moons, like Create + Cultivate, The Newsette and Thrive Global. The truth is, if I can do this, you can too. I simply built up my credibility in the media by never taking for granted any single opportunity to get my name out there. I know that if I keep building my Orion's Roadmap following this strategy, more doors will continue to unlock. And hopefully, one day soon, Savannah Guthrie will be standing behind one of them.

JESSICA'S ORION'S ROADMAP™

The Today Show!!!

ORION'S STAR

Create + Cultivate   *The Newsette*   *Thrive Global*

MOONS

The Jam   *Lux + Concord*   *Fox 32*   *The Glu*   *A Sweat Life*

PLANETS

CHARTING THE COURSE

Now that you understand the mechanism of Orion's Roadmap, let's build yours, as this will be the foundation to the next critical step: pitching, outreach, and booking your speaking engagements, podcast interviews, blog features, and media placements!

As a way to mitigate the overwhelm that comes with Pandora's Box of External Outreach options, I recommend choosing one "type" of media to focus on.

So for example, if your Orion's Star is to be a keynote speaker at a major conference, start to identify local, regional, and national conferences that are looking for speakers and panelists. Based on size and reach, begin to categorize them into the different respective Planet and Moon categories. If you are aiming for a national TV spot as your Orion's Star, what are the local and regional TV shows and even web shows that you can categorize into your Planets and Moons?

Over time, you can start to diversify your External Outreach strategy, blending different types of platforms to create one comprehensive strategy in order to generate as much awareness as possible. However, for the purposes of beginning, I want you to stay laser focused on charting the course to your Orion's Star. Remember, when you try to be everything to everyone, you end up becoming nothing to no one.

When it comes to researching where to find potential Planets and Moons, turn to Google, social media, and sources like Alexa.com and SiteWorthTraffic.com. Don't overthink this part. Chances are, you already have an idea of the sites, stages, and publications you would like to be featured on. Use those as your jumping-off point and make a running list of your Planets, Moons, and Stars. The lists for your Planets and Moons should be exhaustive, as you will revisit this list in a few short pages.

Now it's time to prioritize these lists based on (1) the hits or opportunities that you want the most and (2) the likelihood of achieving these hits based on connections or relationships you might have or perhaps the clear track record this platform has in featuring people similar to you. (I call these low barriers to entry.) You'll then plug in your Planets and Moons to chart the course as you go forth and pitch yourself to the media.

Now that you know where you are going, how are you going to get there? How are you *actually* going to get yourself on that stage in front of thousands, or on that online publication blasted to hundreds of thousands, or in a newsroom broadcasted to millions?

Spoiler alert: you simply have to ask.

With intention, of course.

YOUR ORION'S ROADMAP™

ORION'S STAR

MOONS

PLANETS

Be.
a star

You deserve to shine.
It's really that simple.

CHAPTER 14

PITCH LIKE A PRO

"Don't sit down and wait for opportunities
to come. Get up and make them."

Madam C. J. Walker

Remember that decision makers—editors, producers, bookers—
are people just like you. Do you like it when people only engage with you
when they want something? Doesn't it make you feel a bit, well, *used*?
The key to creating opportunities for yourself starts with creating relationships. You can break through to these folks by starting with an offer
versus opening with a request. Study what they write about or produce
and find ways to add value to their work first before asking them to promote yours . . . especially if they have no idea who you are.

The second way of securing a placement is perfecting your pitch.

Warning: you *will* get rejected. Sometimes you're not even rejected;
you're downright ignored. You have to accept that, for some time, a
large majority of your pitching will fall on deaf ears and you'll get crick-
ets. It doesn't matter. Believe in yourself enough to keep going. Plus, by
now, you've established a running list of potential outlets that should
continue to fuel your outreach. And remember: *a rejection is simply a
redirection.* There is always something out there better for you.

Before we go into constructing the perfect pitch, let's level set on what a pitch actually is. Your pitch is a personalized email strategy. That's it! It's not only about what you send, but when, to whom, and how often.

Let's take a look at the perfect pitch-letter framework, which always includes four elements: (1) something relevant or timely (2) credibility, (3) an element of exclusivity, and (4) a clear call to action.

Here's my pitch letter, which you can use as an example to help you build yours.

Now that you have an understanding of what elements to include, craft your pitch letter. Additionally, get clear on your ask and what aspects of your work point to your credibility. And remember, your ask should exhibit an offering of value, versus a one-way request for yourself.

FINDING THE RIGHT CONTACT

Where might you assume the media are finding their information and inspiration for news stories these days?

A recent survey from Zeno and Muck Rack (two of the PR industry's leading firms) shows that reporters and journalists are turning to social media as their primary news source, and consider the social media "shareability" of an idea before covering it.[1] And, not surprisingly, building authentic relationships still reigns supreme.

This is amazing news for you. Flash back to just a decade or so ago: if you wanted to directly connect with the media, you would have to hire a PR firm and spend thousands of dollars for them to "represent you" in order to do so. You can still do that, of course. But the beauty is you don't need to. With the power of Google and the advent of social media, all you need today is a dose of direction and a dash of gumption.

Let's turn to Twitter. Twitter is a listening tool, prime for politics, celebrity and . . . the media. In fact, the biggest proportion of "verified users" (meaning the accounts with the little blue checkmarks, i.e., legit accounts) are assorted media folks. Think journalists, contributors, news producers, anchors, TV show hosts, and so on. Collectively, they

JESSICA'S PITCH

Hi <Insert Contact's Name>,

TIMELINESS →

In today's fledgling workforce economy, a single job listing attracts on average more than 200 resumes. So, how do you stand out in today's saturated space? Simple: by developing a compelling personal brand that helps you shine above the rest to potential employers and I would love to help you do just that.

CREDIBILITY →

Who am I? My name is Jessica Zweig. I am an award-winning personal branding expert and the Founder & CEO of SimplyBe., a premier personal branding company empowering the world's biggest thought leaders and brands, including Google, Pinterest, Salesforce, and Virgin. My professional accomplishments have gained extreme praise with *Inc.*, hailing me a "Top Digital Marketer to Watch," *Forbes* naming me a "Personal Branding Expert," and one of the *Chicago Tribune's* top "10 Entrepreneurs to Follow."

EXCLUSIVITY →

My easy, expert strategies will empower your audience to position themselves as thought leaders in their respective industries, build connections, and develop a brand people will not forget. I would love to share a select handful of my proprietary trademarked formulas with your audience for tangible takeaways on how they can build their own brands. These are the same formulas I provide for my Fortune 500 clients.

Here's the deal: everyone has a personal brand, and it's more important now than ever to properly define that brand in order to establish credibility and set yourself apart from the competition.

CTA +SIGN-OFF →

For reference, you can find my media kit here for your consideration. I look forward to hearing your thoughts.

With light,
Jessica Zweig

represent almost a quarter of the verified accounts on Twitter. Check out the following graph[2]:

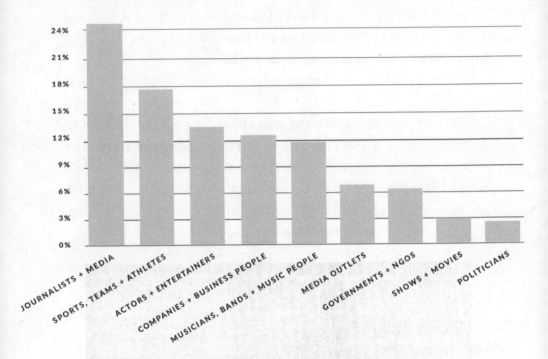

My friends, this is a PR gold mine! By spending just a few minutes each day or even each week, you can directly reach out to the actual media with a click of a button.

In that sense, when it comes to your External Outreach strategy, Twitter trumps any other social media platform. It even dominates Google. Why?

Enter the power of the DM, or direct message. On this channel, you have the ability to not only search decision makers in the world of all media but to directly interact with them in real time. Before you do, I recommend that you pay attention to their feeds and strategically engage with their tweets. This means "like" (signified by a heart icon) the tweets that resonate and "retweet" their posts that you feel would have value for your own following. I call this the Law of the Boomerang, and we will cover it in depth in the next chapter. For now, remember that you have to "give to get." In order to receive a "yes" to a request for an opportunity from an editor, journalist, or producer, you have to earn it. You can't just slide into a stranger's DM and ask for a favor. Establish a relationship first by demonstrating you have invested time in who they are and the work they're doing in the world.

Now that you know the Twitter rules of the road, let's find the right contacts.

Say you're a fitness expert, and your Orion's Star is to land a feature in *Shape* magazine. Head on over to Twitter and find the search bar, toggle to "People" and type in, "Shape magazine editor." (I recommend searching the title "editor" over "contributor," as editors are the folks who usually hold decision-making powers.) The results that would appear in a search today are as follows:

In just one search, you have not only discovered editors at *Shape* magazine but additionally, editors and writers who work for other magazines in the same wheelhouse like *Women's Health*, *GQ*, and *Furthermore*. Cha-ching! With these people identified, here are the six action steps, or what we like to call the "Self-Pitch Six," you would need to take:

1. Follow them.
2. Scan their feeds and "heart" any tweets you connect with.
3. Over the course of the next few weeks, pay close attention to their feeds and "retweet" and respond to at least three to five tweets per week, while continuing to "heart" the others that resonate.
4. Pay attention. This act will inevitably get you on their radar, and you most likely will see them follow you back and begin to engage with your activity in return.
5. After a few weeks of interaction, send them a DM formally introducing yourself. In this first introduction, DO NOT ASK FOR ANYTHING. Just say hi and compliment their work. Chances are they'll respond with a quick thank you. Don't get discouraged if they don't respond. Your first message shouldn't warrant a response. You're simply sending them some appreciation.
6. Repeat steps 1 through 4 once more. At this stage, you are primed to reach out and introduce your work, your content, and your idea and politely ask for their consideration in featuring you.

The Self-Pitch Six, and the overarching philosophy behind its approach, applies broadly across all social media channels, including Instagram, Facebook, and LinkedIn. But since we're in the business of connecting with people who command the power of new exposure for your brand, Twitter is your best bet when you're focused on this part of your strategy.

But in the event you can't find what you're looking for on Twitter, you can always head on over to good ol' faithful Google and search your target platforms directly there. Once you're on their websites, search either their "About" sections. Or often they provide a "Contact" section with direct information to submit yourself.

This task of scouring Twitter and Google on the regular to identify contacts will, over time, evolve into a customized media list. As you build yours out, and as your outreach continues to evolve, you're going to need to stay committed. This is a good opportunity to tap your accountability partner for some extra support. After all, the art of securing placements isn't a one-time event but an ongoing, living, breathing effort. Remember, it's rare to receive a response from an editor, journalist, producer, or conference booker on the first go. It's essential you pound the proverbial PR pavement on an ongoing basis using the SimplyBe. External Outreach Approach. If I could pound the *literal* pavement, knocking on doors with postcards in hand all across the great city of Chicago all those years ago when I started my magazine, you can spend a few hours in front of your computer each week building out one of the most effective steps in raising the awareness of your brand.

A MEDIA KIT: THE CHERRY ON TOP

Over the course of your ongoing External Outreach, if you're following the formulas, the chances of you accumulating PR opportunities are high. Imagine, as you start to build your platform with custom Pinnacle Content and build a tribe on social media, you begin to secure blog features, a couple of panel talks, and a podcast interview. And that's only the beginning! You need to capture it, package it, and leverage it.

Enter the media kit, a powerful asset in your brand perception, especially in the eyes of the media. For starters, it's an instant credibility builder, as it innately suggests you take your own work as a thought leader seriously. Secondly, it's a tool that gives you a leading edge since . . . well . . . not everyone makes time to put together a polished,

Jessica
ZWEIG

CEO + FOUNDER, **SimplyBe.**

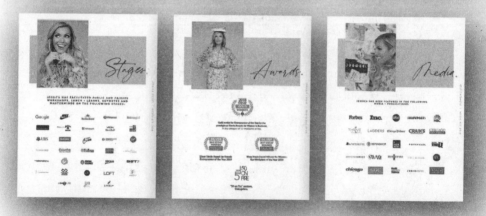

thoughtful, and clear media kit. The mere fact that *you* do helps you to stand out even more. And finally, it adds an element of polish to your pitch email by streamlining your message and all your past work into one clarified asset.

Usually, a media kit comes in the form of a branded, well-designed PDF that includes the following key elements:

- *A professional headshot*
- *A short-form bio*
- *Your "signature topics," which can be translated by way of a keynote talk, a bylined article, a podcast interview, or a media feature*
- *Your past "hits," which are best displayed by showcasing on one page all the logos of the different platforms you have been featured on, as well as potential screenshots of your best features*
- *A spotlight on your platform; think: your podcast, web show, course program, or more information on your company, including client testimonials or awards you've won*
- *Your contact information, as well as your social handles*

For some media kit inspiration, mine is on the next page.

Remember, no matter where you are in your career, or what industry you're in, you can use the media kit "formula" to showcase your work and enhance your perception.

At this point, you might be thinking that you're going to need to hire some fancy shmancy, expensive designer to make it beautiful. Fret not, my friend. I recommend using Canva, a simple to use, surprisingly powerful and flexible graphic design tool. It's no Photoshop, but it can do a lot of basic design tasks quite efficiently using drag and drop.

IT'S SHOWTIME

You have identified your Orion's Star, done your due diligence on your Planets and Moons, and charted the course. You've perfected your pitch letter and spent hours engaging on Twitter and researching on Google and even more time working on the pitches and follow-ups themselves.

To boot, you have kept yourself organized and on track along the way, accelerating this part of your strategy and thus, your time.

And now . . . you've scored the hit, secured the speaking engagement, booked the interview, and nabbed the byline. (Remember, it doesn't take perfection to be successful at this game. It simply takes persistence.)

Brava, my friend.

But what now? Did you anticipate the yes? Maybe you did, maybe you didn't. Know that the act of pitching yourself is only 50 percent of the game. The other 50 percent is actually SHOWING UP, fully prepared, fully YOU. It sounds simpler than it is, but the truth is, you only get one shot. Not to sound like a Debbie Downer, but if you mess up that first live TV interview on that local talk show or bomb that first keynote at your dream conference or send over an ill-informed, poorly written article to an esteemed news outlet, the chances of them asking you back are slim to none.

And you wanna get asked back!

You didn't work this hard to be a one-hit wonder. Additionally, you want to be able to proudly leverage that particular feature, video segment, or opportunity not only to get asked back but to open up more doors for more exposure. You want to be able to put that feature in your media kit, and share it with the world.

The point? Preparation is everything. Here's what you need to do:

- *Dress for success: We are going to spend a lot of time talking about the power of clothing in a few short chapters from now, but suffice to say that what you wear, especially on camera, on stage, or even for a first meeting with an editor, matters. This doesn't make you vain. This makes you strategic. Your clothes tell a story, and you're making a first impression. Would you go on a hot date in dirty laundry? Of course you wouldn't. Dress to impress, my friend. It's all your brand.*

- *Practice: You didn't come this far to sound like a hack. If you're giving a keynote talk or being interviewed on a TV show or a podcast, you should know your talking points. Don't expect to rely on your innate understanding of your topic. You can pretty much guarantee you'll feel the butterflies and you run the risk of blanking. (It happens to the best of us.) The more you practice, the better you'll come across. Stick the landing.*

- *Research: Do your due diligence. Go in knowing as much as you can about the host, the interviewer, the writer, and most of all, the community, following, attendees, or readership. How can you cater your content to fit their needs, and what questions can you come prepared with, so that you generate an engaging, two-way conversation versus a cut-and-dried interview? When you do your research, the taller and more grounded you stand, the richer, more valuable piece of content you provide for the audience of the platform. Remember it's all about delivering value.*

- *Send a thank-you note: There's nothing classier than a good old-fashioned, handwritten thank-you note, sent via snail mail. The truth is, being featured in a magazine, on a podcast, at a conference, or on a TV show has given your career a tremendous gift. Acknowledge that. Sometimes the simplest acts of kindness are the most profound. I have been told point blank by producers and journalists that the reason they asked me back onto their show or blog was because I left such a positive impression with a thank-you note. #truestory*

Once your feature is publicly available, share it like crazy. This is perhaps one of the most important and *powerful* benefits to achieving External Outreach exposure. Resharing your PR hits elevates the perception of your brand. This further establishes you as the expert in your space and thus increases your market value.

There's no shame in spinning your own story and leveraging all this newfound exposure for credibility, greater recognition, and respect. Because the truth is, the brighter you shine, the more people you reach. And the more people you reach, the more people you can serve.

CRAFTING YOUR PITCH

TIMELINESS $\longrightarrow$

CREDIBILITY $\longrightarrow$

EXCLUSIVITY $\longrightarrow$

CTA +SIGN-OFF $\longrightarrow$

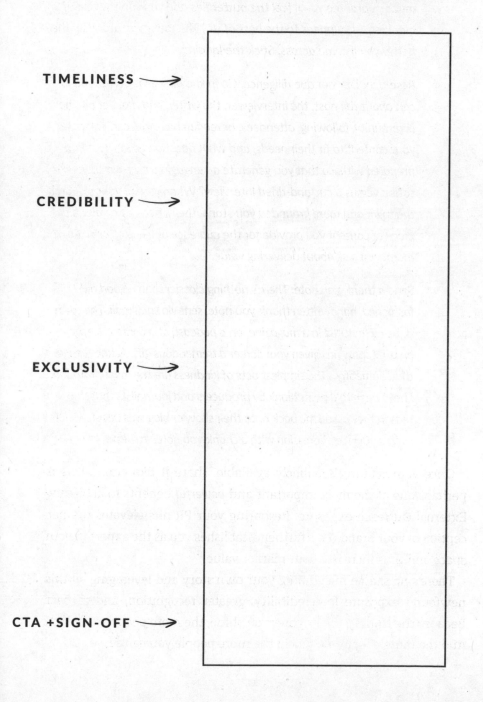

Be.

a magnet

If you do not believe you deserve
recognition, accolades, awards, spotlight,
and success, no one else will. You must
first decide you are worth it. It is only
when you align yourself to the vibration
and embodiment of worth that you
attract the opportunities you seek.
This is how dreams become a reality.

CHAPTER 15

GET YOUR (SOCIAL MEDIA) MIND RIGHT

"Being famous on Instagram is almost the
same thing as being rich in Monopoly."

Anonymous

I was in the right place at the right time.

Flashback again to the spring of 2008, when I was still a struggling actress, working multiple day jobs to pay rent. One of those jobs just so happened to be at a gym. Since I was too broke to afford a membership, I got a gig working the front desk so I could work out for free. (A girl's gotta do what a girl's gotta do.)

It was at that gig that I met my future business partner. One evening, we were on one of our usual dinner dates and scheming ideas for Cheeky when she casually mentioned how she loved using this thing called Facebook to see who was dating whom and to stay in touch with her friends from college.

I'll never forget going home that night to my vintage, North Side Chicago apartment, making a beeline for my laptop, and popping open my browser. I vividly remember typing in "www.facebook.com" for the very first time and registering my account.

From the second I joined Facebook, I instinctively understood it. Its potential hit me like a tidal wave. This was *not* a place that I was going to keep up with friends from high school to see who got married when. This was a portal into a free audience for my magazine. This was the best marketing tool ever invented. This was a global megaphone. This was an untapped, unlimited community. This was a freakin' window onto the world.

The early days of Facebook were a wide-open playing field. No one fully understood what it was yet, let alone how to maximize it. Since my intention was to promote Cheeky, I had an innate knack for Facebook posts by translating marketing lingo into authentic, conversational, quippy copy.

What's more, Cheeky began to throw consistent parties, and at each event, we had photographers come out to capture the experience. I quickly learned the power of pictures and how much people love to devour them. I would upload our events into "Albums," and awareness naturally started to grow around our brand.

I also decided that, as my experience with Facebook evolved and Cheeky began to gain momentum, I would accept and request "friends" not from a personal standpoint, but from a strategic one. I had two rules: (1) since I was running a women's lifestyle magazine, I accepted practically any female users that would send me a friend request and (2) if you were a male user and we had more than twenty mutual connections in common, I would also accept your request. (I did my best to avoid the creepsters and still do.)

Over the course of those early few years on Facebook, I grew my friend count to close to five thousand. When the topic of Facebook came up in social settings, and I mentioned this number in conversation, I'd get a slightly snide, "Oh, don't you think you're special" look. But the truth is, I never attempted to amass a big community on Facebook as a vanity play. I did it purely as a business strategy. Because having a large, and more importantly, engaged audience was fucking *magical*.

It went like this: The more I produced valuable, *compelling* content on Facebook's feed, the more my potential readers would get a taste of what my brand was all about. The more I responded to my audience's comments on that content, the better the ability I had to create real relationships with them online, and therefore offline. The more *consistent* I was with my communication with them, the more loyal they would become to me and the brand. As a result, city-wide awareness started to build on Facebook about Cheeky, word of mouth started to grow, and my site traffic skyrocketed. And the more audience I had on my own website, the more money I could charge advertisers in my magazine to reach that community.

It was this beautiful equation of tactics, approach, and results that had a domino effect on the success of my business. The equation went like this:

- *Great content + sincere engagement = authentic relationships*
- *Authentic relationships + consistency = loyalty*
- *Loyalty + growth = revenue*

Over the course of the past decade and a half, these core principles of how social media works have not changed. People think they have, because there are so many new channels now with different algorithms, features, tools, and "best practices." You can bet your Facebook stock options that between the time you start this book and finish it, something else in the social media macrocosm will have changed. It's impossible to keep up with every single channel, platform, update, hack, hashtag, and expert spewing data.

I'm here to tell you: you don't need to.

Social media is a gift in today's business world. It allows you to connect with people from across the planet with a push of a button and establish actual relationships with actual human beings—if you're willing to tell, not sell, and stay authentic. This didn't exist just twenty years ago, and it has facilitated new business growth in an unprecedented capacity at a global scale. If you want to crush it on social media today, tomorrow, and in the years to come, keep it real, be in service, and stay authentic.

Remember: They don't call it "advertising media" or "marketing media" or "business media." They call it *social* media, as it's intended for you to harness the power of authentic connection so that you can build REAL relationships. Because relationships are the life source of all business, no matter what industry you are in.

But before you go forth to build a robust social strategy, let's get honest with our feelings about social media in the first place.

IT'S COMPLICATED

Pop quiz: What adjectives come to mind when you hear the words *social media*?

- *Brilliant?*
- *Overwhelming?*
- *Confusing?*
- *Exciting?*
- *Infuriating?*
- *Annoying?*
- *Dangerous?*
- *Amazing?*
- *Inspiring?*

- *Helpful?*
- *Evil?*
- *Anxiety inducing?*
- *Fun?*
- *Obsessive?*
- *Dumb?*
- *Addictive?*
- *Distracting?*
- *Essential?*

Perhaps you resonated with all the words on this list, just some of them, or none at all. Perhaps you have your own laundry list of descriptive terms you could draw out when you hear those two little words. Suffice to say, for most of us, our relationship with social media is complicated.

Let's call a spade a spade. We cannot deny that social media has perpetuated a mass era of anxiety, depression, bullying, toxicity, oversexualization, trolls, corruption, stalking, anger, and negativity never before experienced by any other generation. The constant barrage of perfectly filtered photos on Instagram alone is bound to knock even the most confident person's self-esteem, while obsessively checking your Twitter feed just before bed contributes toward poor-quality sleep. Teenagers who spend more than three hours a day on social media have double the risk of mental health problems than those who don't.[1] And the average American checks their phone eighty times a day.[2]

Some might call the impact social media has had on our current culture and society a downright epidemic. I believe that's only true if *you* allow it to be. The truth is, just like with everything in the universe, you have free will. And just like everything in your own life, you have to take responsibility for your own actions, choices, and responses. That said, you completely control and curate your own unique social media experience.

Personally, I love my experience on social media. Why? No, it's not because I am in the business of marketing and therefore biased. It's because I know I get to CHOOSE who I follow and who I engage with, what I create, what I share, what I consume, how much time I spend on my phone, and most of all, what my intention is in using social media in the first place. I am fully responsible for my own relationship with social media.

So are you.

My intention as a content creator on social media is to to motivate, captivate, and illuminate my audience through empowerment and positivity. Therefore, my intention as a content *consumer* is to find people who do the same thing for me. It's that simple. Anything or anyone that doesn't fit that description simply does not make its way into my feeds. And if and when something other than empowering, inspiring, or positive content somehow sneaks its way in for whatever reason, I unfollow, mute, unfriend, block, and sometimes, simply put my phone down for extended periods of time. These aforementioned acts are not rude or even toxic in and of themselves. They are acts of self-love and self-preservation.

This has been my approach to social media since the first minute I spent on Facebook back in 2008, and it still stands to this day. This decision alone has grown my business (and to be fair, my life) tremendously. I met my best friends, built my network, got set up with my husband, found my dream team of employees, and scaled a seven-figure business with the support of social media.

And I'm not the only one that this kind of thing is happening to. I see the same thing happening for the people I admire and aspire to be like in my own career. The people who are winning on social media are the ones who are harnessing it for good. When I pop open my Instagram, I see accounts like Lori Harder, Lalah Delia, Danielle LaPorte, Layla Saad, Alexandra Roxo, Sah D'Simone, Lacy Phillips, Lauren Ash, Chinae Alexander, Luvvie Ajayi Jones, Sahara Rose, Shaman Durek, Hilary Rushford, and Gala Darling.

These are the people who are transforming and transmuting the negative complexities of the social media space and using their platforms as havens for community, service, authenticity, and love. They are the content creators who motivate, captivate, and illuminate with every piece they share and every person they engage with. Not so coincidentally, they are the people who are growing mass followings, shifting their industries, building real relationships with other influential people, and growing their businesses (and platforms) beyond what would have been possible just a few short years ago as a result.

When you open your social media accounts, who do you see? Are they inspiring you, touching your heart, motivating you, or simply making you smile?

When people open their accounts and see YOU, what do they see?

I challenge you to reframe the potential stigmas you might have around social media and intentionally choose to look at it in a new way. I challenge you to curate your own user experience and take full responsibility for it. Ask yourself what kind of content you wish to consume and what kind of content you want to create. *You* can become one of those people who grows a mass following while changing the perception of social media. You can be the person who uses it as a positive investment in the future—not just of your business but of the world.

It's all a choice.

PEOPLE > POPULARITY

Alright, you're clear that you will show up fully authentic, purely positive, and in total service to your audience.

However, social media can still feel overwhelming. That's because people get so lost in the next best platform, discouraged by the latest algorithm change, distracted by the fancy new feature, or most of all, obsessed with follower count that they miss the whole damn point.

That's the micro shit. Let's zoom out and focus on the macro. The big picture. The vast, wide-open opportunity that you have at this very moment by the mere fact you've got your smartphone in your hand. This opportunity is called *connection*. You can build a business *and* a genuine community at the same time. Meaning when you build your social media strategy, the fourth and final component of your Pinnacle Content Framework, you must use your business mind *and* your human heart. They are not mutually exclusive, and the more you blend the two, the greater chances of success.

Social media is the number one place to connect and cultivate a tribe of real people. It doesn't matter if you reach ten human beings or a million. Each and every one of them matters because they are living, breathing, feeling souls just like you and just like me. Don't underestimate the power of a niche community.

But, there is no denying it. Having an engaged social media following is one of the most invaluable forms of currency anyone aiming for thought leadership can possess. It increases your credibility and opens up doors to the media, speaking engagements, and better clients and ultimately can help you command more revenue for your time, services, products, and even your presence.

Who wouldn't want a thriving, growing, and engaged audience?

However, there are two hugely common mistakes happening all over social media and the subsequent effort to grow an audience. The first mistake is letting the "need to be seen" take the wheel. What I mean by this is focusing solely on the numbers. In today's world of building and monetizing a personal brand, you don't need a million followers to make a million dollars. You can, in fact, make an incredible living with a thousand followers who truly care about your brand.

I've walked this talk. As I write this book, I have a decent number of followers on Instagram, with around sixty thousand actual people who dig my content. Now, in Instagram terms, that's a relatively niche audience. I am certainly not reaching millions of people. At least not yet. And with Instagram's latest algorithm updates, it's been harder and harder for me to reach them. On a good day, I am only able to reach 10 percent of them, which is about six thousand people.

Have I cursed and blamed Instagram? Actually, no. Have I let it stop me from consistently, constantly, and clearly sharing value with my community? Hell to the no. Has it prevented me from using it to try to monetize my audience? Nope. And has it prohibited me from reaping amazing financial and critical success? Negative.

Case in point: SimplyBe.'s live Masterclasses. These are events I open to the public, where I teach the SimplyBe. methodology over the course of a two-day experience to a small audience. I charge roughly $1,000 per ticket for these events, as they are chock-full of our proprietary tools and are phenomenally produced events to boot. I work hard to promote these events for three straight months, across all of social media. My very first one resulted in a sold-out event of fifty attendees. (Some who flew into Chicago from other states around the United States, and even a small number who flew in from Europe!)

On the morning of the first day of the Masterclass, I asked the room by a show of hands how many had heard of the event through my Instagram. Over 95 percent of the room raised their arms high in the sky. By now, you've done the math and know that that Masterclass was a $50,000 weekend for SimplyBe. What I want to point out is that it all came down to fifty people. That's less than 1 percent of my audience on Instagram. That's all I needed to buy in and say yes to my product. I knew they had all showed up and invested in themselves not because I *sold* to them for those few months of promotion. It was because I *spoke* to them.

And I didn't let the algorithm or an obsession with follower count get in my way. You shouldn't either.

This leads me to the second mistake of treating your online community like they are just numbers. Or rather, "likes" or "hearts" or "reshares." These are real human beings we're talking about. Real people with real needs, real problems, and real emotions. The second you start regarding each and every one of them as such, your ability to truly connect with them will shift, and so will your growth and engagement.

With this newfound understanding in mind, let's revisit the final section of your Pinnacle Content Framework: Social Media Amplification. Since the landscape of social media changes by the minute, we're going to focus not on the specific channel tactics but on the overarching, surefire principles that will work regardless of channel, content type, follower total, or year in time you are executing your strategy.

Eat your heart out, TikTok.

Be.

genuine

Would you rather have 1,000 pennies or 100 dollars? Value your people, and they will value you. Their attention, after all, is your most precious currency.

CHAPTER 16

THE TEN EVERGREEN PRINCIPLES OF SOCIAL MEDIA

"The sea changes color,
but the sea does not change."

Stevie Nicks

There are no shortcuts to building an authentic personal brand. It's not about being timely as much as it is about being timeless.

The same applies to your social media platforms. Something that is fast, fleeting, and ephemeral is not the aim. You want to keep your approach to this part of your strategy "evergreen." In marketing speak, *evergreen* means "products, segments, and strategies that stay relevant over a long period of time."

Introducing the Ten Evergreen Principles of Social Media:

1. Quality
2. Consistency
3. Partnerships
4. Boomerang
5. Nurturing

6. Accessibility
7. Tact
8. Compounding
9. Integration
10. Fun

These principles are designed to not only stand the test of time but to power your growth and success on social media *right now*. This is about establishing the long-term mindset you must have when it comes to building your most valuable form of digital currency: your audience. Sure, you can go out and buy the latest book on Instagram influencer strategy or shop the latest course on Facebook ads or download the latest podcast on YouTube virality, but six months from now, it will all be outdated. You can certainly skip all the courses and just go hire a growth hacker, invest in a GrowthBot, or do a loop giveaway. Perhaps you don't even know what the heck I'm talking about . . . no? My point exactly.

Shortsighted tactics, channel-specific tools, bot software, and growth hacks come and go. And if you do that shit, so will your audience. These approaches aren't authentic, let alone sustainable, and your audience will grow faux. Adopting these Evergreen Principles will enable you to build an authentic audience, while driving your long-term success, which is what you're ultimately aiming for. Today's growth hack is tomorrow's pleather bag from the fast-fashion outlet. By next season it's already out of style. The Evergreen Principles are like designer handbags: sustainable, timeless, and built to last.

Apply these principles, and you will grow on social media, no matter how much the landscape changes. Which it will.

Here we go.

THE PRINCIPLE OF QUALITY

When I was about to launch Cheeky, I flew to New York City to network. On a whim, I had gotten a meeting with Dany Levy, the founder of DailyCandy, which had become the largest daily newsletter platform for young women from 2000 to 2008. About six months prior to my meeting with her, Dany had sold DailyCandy to Comcast for the sum of $125 million. #NBD.

Needless to say, getting a face-to-face meeting with her was nothing short of a fucking miracle. I had to hedge my questions strategically.

Naturally, my very first (and most important) question for her was, "How do I monetize my magazine?"

I assumed she would explain how advertisers pay more money for larger audiences and would have thus guided me on how to grow my audience too. I'll never forget what she said instead: "Focus on the quality of your content. That's all you need to do."

I was confused and inquired for a bit more information. She continued by reiterating, "Build a beautiful platform. Produce amazing content. Do that, and your readers will come. When the readers come, so will the advertisers. But don't build your brand for them. Build your brand for the women who need your message, not the advertisers looking to capitalize on them. Give them a reason to care. That is how you will make money."

This was single-handedly the best piece of professional advice I have ever received. It's been a guiding principle along every step of my career. To this day, I focus not only on the quality of my content but also the quality (not quantity) of my audience. I have seen time and time again how a thousand people who give a shit about your brand trumps having a hundred thousand who don't care.

When you focus on the numbers, it's your ego talking, and you can leave it at the door. Focus on the *quality* of your content and the *quality* of your audience, and you will always win. Hey, you might even win $125 million. As I keep telling you, anything is possible.

THE PRINCIPLE OF CONSISTENCY

We've talked about the power of consistency a lot. But second to consistent messaging, nowhere does it matter more in your digital presence than in your consistent social media activity.

Let's first address *cadence*. You can't expect to "hit it hard" for three months on Instagram, dip out and chill for two months because of #life, then tap back in for another month, only to disappear again for another six weeks, and expect to grow. The part of the Pinnacle Content Framework here is called Social Media Amplification via

Weekly Communication. Now, weekly doesn't mean daily. I personally don't believe posting every day is sustainable or necessary. But you *do* need to show up on whatever platforms you choose—whether that be LinkedIn, Facebook, Instagram, Twitter, Snapchat, or Pinterest—three to five times per week, week after week.

You also need consistency in your *presence*. Ideally, you have the same brand name on all your social channels, meaning your Twitter handle is the same as your Instagram handle, and the URLs to your Facebook, LinkedIn, and Pinterest all match up to your brand name and Twitter and Instagram handles: that is linkedin.com/jessicazweig, instagram. com/jessicazweig and pinterest.com/jessicazweig. This is how you not only become easily found in a search (a HUGE benefit for growth) but also easily identified as your brand name (a huge plus for brand recognition and brand perception).

Finally, you want consistency in your social media *bios*. Every single one of your social media channels has an "About," "Bio," or "Summary" section, and it is one of the most invaluable pieces of real estate on your entire personal brand platform. You want to ensure the messaging here is the same, so you're always telling one consistent, clear, and cohesive story. Go back to your Hologram Headline as well as your Brand Pillars and even use your Supernova for inspiration on implementing a consistent message across all of your channels. Finally, use the same professional, clear, and recent headshot across all your social bios for that extra level of polish and unmistakable recognition and consistency.

THE PRINCIPLE OF PARTNERSHIPS

One of the most effective ways to grow your own audience is to get in front of other audiences. This is a seriously effective version of "off-site events." The first step is identifying partners to cocreate a partnership with. Now, *partnerships* is a loaded word today on social media. Whether we're talking about brand partnerships or influencer partnerships, it can all feel a tad overwhelming and invoke a bit of imposter syndrome. Let's ditch the current narrative on the word *partnership* and start fresh.

You don't need to be a mega fashion influencer, a food blogger, or a celebrity to build super powerful partnerships on social media. Everyone in your immediate social sphere (and even beyond it) is a potential partner. If they (or you) have a smaller audience, don't underestimate it. The "riches are in the niches," as I like to say. When choosing a partner, ask yourself the following questions:

- *Does this person or brand share the same values as me?*
- *Does this person or brand have a like-minded message?*
- *Are we in differing, complementary, or identical industries?*
- *How could these differences or similarities creatively impact our partnership?*

Once you've gotten clear on who your potential partners could be, the second step is to simply reach out and ask! A great place to start is within your own peer group, friends, and community. But in the event you want to partner with someone you don't know, go for it. You never know if you don't try, and if you don't ask, you're practically guaranteed a no. And if you do reach out to that said "dream" partner, and they do in fact say no, guess what? That's the worst of it! You're still alive, right? Remember, a rejection is simply a redirection.

Your third step, once you've agreed to partner, is to define together what the partnership will actually entail. Remember, this is all about sharing value. Organic partnerships on social media can come in many forms, including but certainly not limited to the following:

- *Cohosted Instagram Lives*
- *Cohosted livestreams on Facebook*
- *An Instagram takeover*
- *A Twitter chat*
- *A cocreated private group on LinkedIn*
- *A cocreated private group or page on Facebook*
- *An "appreciation" post on LinkedIn, tagging each other's work and sharing why you value it*

- *Simply sharing photos of one another on Facebook or Instagram and tagging one another's accounts*

The nature of the partnership itself doesn't matter, as long as you both agree to the terms of cross promotion (remember, the aim is to get seen by new audiences and therefore *grow*). And most of all, you want to ensure that you're creating motivating, captivating, or illuminating content for your respective audiences. Deliver value, and you will always win.

THE PRINCIPLE OF THE BOOMERANG

Having been on social media for years, I've made a lot of social media "friends"—meaning people I have never actually met in person. I had one particularly emphatic connection on LinkedIn named Megan, a fellow marketing entrepreneur. From the moment she began following me, she would reshare practically every post I published. I would comment on those reshared posts with a quick "thank you!" However, simply commenting back didn't seem like enough. Her support of my content was so genuine and so consistent, I wanted to return the favor. And so I began to pay closer attention to Megan's LinkedIn channel and learned to love *her* content on marketing too. I started sharing her content on my feed, as I genuinely believed it would resonate with my own audience. (I also did it to show my reciprocity.) Within a few short weeks of resharing Megan's content, I received an InMail message from her, asking if she could have my personal email as she wanted to introduce me to one of her colleagues who was looking for a speaker on personal branding. That connection not only turned into one of the highest-paid speaking engagements of my career, but I also received multiple clients from that very event.

They say what goes around comes around. This isn't just karma, it's a smart social media strategy. Welcome to the Principle of the Boomerang. Yes, we all want our content to get seen, heard, and commented on. Newsflash: so does everyone else. When was the last time you spent time on your social apps purely to comment, like, and share other's work? This tiny act of giving can reap massive rewards.

Learn to pay it forward, appreciate your audience, and be generous with your time. These microactions of giving back on social can lead to macro results in your business.

THE PRINCIPLE OF NURTURING

Most people are so focused on building a following that they forget to focus on the one they already have. Let's face it, the saturation of content creators, influencers, and sheer users has made it harder than ever to grow on any social channel. Instead of obsessing about follower count (also known as vanity metrics), focus on your follower engagement. You do this through nurturing your followers. *Nurture* quite literally means "to care for, cherish, help, and encourage the growth or development of."

Assume you will never grow another follower on social. Assume that your current followers are the only people who will ever engage with, and therefore invest in, your brand. Wouldn't you then treat them as though they were your most precious asset? Guess what? *They are.* Treat them that way and watch how your engagement and eventually your audience ultimately expand. When you're constantly on the hunt for the next follower, your existing community can feel it. Subconsciously they are thinking to themselves, "Hey, what about me?"

When you are in the energy of true service, through creating content that is catered to the audience that is currently following you, they can feel that too. What this looks like is content that doesn't sell to them but rather tells them stories, asks them questions, invites them into your life, polls them for what they like and don't like, responds to their answers, and implements their feedback.

By stepping out of the rat race of growth and instead focusing on service and gratitude, your entire social media experience begins to shift from being a place to compete to a place to build a community. And therein lies all the difference in the (social media) world.

THE PRINCIPLE OF ACCESSIBILITY

A few years ago, I stumbled upon Nicole Arbour, a hilarious comedian, on Instagram. She was blond, funny as hell, whip-smart, uber sexy, mega successful, and clearly empowered. She made no apologies for who she was, what she looked like, and what she had to say—even if it was socially or politically polarizing, which it often was. Her confidence resonated with me. I saw myself in her in a lot of ways, so I began to follow her. Over time, I became a fan. I would frequently comment on her posts with quick encouragement and kudos. She never responded to my comments but by no means did I mind or expect her to. The girl has millions of followers on Instagram. I knew my semi-regular commentary was just a drop in the bucket.

After a few months of my following her/fangirling her, she posted a politically charged post that I vehemently disagreed with. It wasn't just angering, it felt like a blindsiding betrayal. How could this woman, whom I so deeply identified with, admired, and had been rooting for for months, have such a polar-opposite view on something that I so deeply believed in my core?

In an emotional reactionary moment, after reading her post, I typed out the comment, "I'm unfollowing you" and hit publish. I had never done that before in my life, and while I admit it was out of character, I felt justified. Within less than sixty seconds, Nicole direct messaged me. Her note read, "Why did you unfollow me?" I was STUNNED. "She knows who I am?" I thought to myself. I responded, hands shaking out of sheer shock, "Because your last post really pissed me off, that's why." She responded again: "I think you misunderstood what I was trying to say."

A fifteen-minute debate via direct message ensued, which concluded with her saying at the end, "It's really important for women like us to have healthy conversations about this stuff, even when we don't agree. I would like you to reconsider following me again. I think you're awesome, I love following you." I couldn't believe it. Not only did she care to hear my perspective and valued my "follow," but she followed me too? I confirmed: "You follow me?" She responded by saying, "Yes, I pay attention to everyone who follows me." Not only did I follow Nicole back, we've since become friends. I even invited her to be my very first guest on The SimplyBe. Podcast, which she promoted to her audience of millions, helping my show to hit the Apple Podcasts charts in my first season.

THIS is the principle (and power) of being accessible. It doesn't matter how big or small your platform is. I believe one of the most beautiful components of all of social media is the mere functionality called the "direct message." No one is too famous, too successful, too important, or, on the flip side, too "unimportant" to reach out to *or* respond to. The simple act of responding can change your business. Maybe your podcast. Potentially even your life.

THE PRINCIPLE OF TACT

Someone once told me a long time ago that the internet is not a place to "process." This feedback came at a time when I was going through a bitter "business divorce." The anger and sadness were immense and sharing my process of pain, revelations, resentment, release, surrender, and so-called "healing" on social media felt wonderfully cathartic. At least to me. To the rest of my community, however, I came across as self-indulgent, self-involved, passive aggressive, and to be frank, un-followable. They were right. I was offering zero value. Thank God I had people in my life willing to tell me the truth and call me out on this shitty behavior and the negative perception that I was unconsciously building around my own platform.

Today, I do believe that the internet (and thereby social media) is a wonderful place to share once we've *completed* our process. When we have truly gone through the fire of fury, sadness, rage, loss, and confusion and have come out on the other side. It is then and only then that we have the newfound clarity, perspective, groundedness, calm, wisdom, and guidance to genuinely glean and share with our audience, in service of *them*—not our own comfort, validation, or attention. To be frank, I find this level of vulnerable honesty in service of a tribe to be some of the best content out there.

It is not only for this reason that you must be mindful of what you share. The internet is written in ink. Yes, there is the ephemeral Snap, the twenty-four-hour Instagram Story, and you can easily delete posts. But the screenshot is real, and you never know who paid attention to the things we shared on our walls, grids, and feeds years ago. It's critical not to let your fury toward politics, your boozy late night out, or your fight with your spouse get the best of you—or your fingers on a touchpad. The Principle of Tact implores you to be conscientious of your brand reputation. This level of consistency—and classiness—in your message will help you grow. Go back to your Hologram, Supernova, and Pinnacle Content. If your bubbling emotional rant doesn't fit the script, take a deep breath and step away from your phone. Your unprocessed emotions don't belong on the holy ground that is your personal brand platform.

THE PRINCIPLE OF COMPOUNDING

We've talked a lot about the noise and saturation of the internet, and how it's harder than ever to cut through it. That doesn't mean you can't. It just means you need to practice patience, stay the course, and be in service. There are no shortcuts to an overnight mass following unless you (1) buy your followers, (2) spend thousands and thousands of dollars in ads, or (3) make it onto *The Bachelor*. Even then, it's a fleeting way to grow an inauthentic audience because you've taken inauthentic steps to acquire them.

When we hear the word *compounding*, we typically think of money. In personal finance, when something compounds, it increases in value by a percentage again and again, over a certain period of time. We can apply the same principle to personal branding on social media. In this case, the longer something (e.g., your audience) sustains itself, the more it increases in value over time. Compounding on social media works like this: *clarity* in your message + *consistency* in your strategy and tactics + *constancy* of time = a large, engaged audience.

The aim is to saturate your own audience with a wide selection of touchpoints. The more you make these touchpoints strategic by way of their quality—the value they deliver and who you're tagging and hashtagging, for instance—the more they will get seen. The longer your practice of distributing rich, organic content, the more your community compounds, or grows.

THE PRINCIPLE OF INTEGRATION

I'll never forget my first meeting with my very first SimplyBe. client, Dana. Dana had found me on the internet, and though we had talked on the phone, this was our very first time working together in person. We were sitting alongside each other, as I was coaching her on her newsletter strategy. Out of the blue, Dana paused, threw down her pen on the table, looked at me with sheer awe, and proclaimed, "Jessica, you are just so INTEGRATED!" I looked at her rather blankly and, somewhat confused, replied, "Thanks . . .?" She went on to say the following, a statement that I will carry with me for the rest of my life: "Who you are on the internet is *exactly* who you are in real life. And if I had met you today for the first time in person and then went and looked you up online, you would be the exact same. You are so integrated."

Ever since then, I've made integration an ongoing goal.

Perhaps you've had the opposite experience, where you meet that person you've been following, admiring, and loving online for years, only to meet them in person and discover they're a total dick. (I certainly have, and there's nothing more crushing.) I bet you unfollowed them too.

The REAL magic of social media happens when you bring your full authentic self to the internet and then let that "personality" shine through evermore offline. I find the most effective way to communicate your authenticity on social media specifically is through the power of real-time video (livestreams and Stories) and clear copy. This can look like emojis, certain punctuation, capital letters, brevity, or verbosity. It doesn't matter. Just be you on social media and ensure that "you" is fully integrated with the "you" who shows up and interacts in real life. The people who follow me online who I have had the pleasure of meeting in person have remained my most engaged, strongest, longest-standing followers. Integration isn't just a reflection of authenticity. It's a growth strategy.

THE PRINCIPLE OF FUN

Gabby Bernstein once said, "Measure your success by how much fun you're having." When it comes to social media, sometimes it can feel anything but fun. The tediousness and overwhelm is real. Instead, I encourage you to look at social media as one big, crazy adventure. It's already changed thousands of times in the past decade and will continue to mutate into its next iteration. You can't control it, you can only ride the wave. So embrace the excitement of change, the newness, and the unknown. Look at every algorithm change, new tool, fun feature, or backend update as an opportunity to PLAY! Appreciate the beautiful ability to connect with strangers from faraway places who have the potential to become friends, colleagues, partners, and clients. Take a look around you and revel in what a privilege it is to live at this current juncture in time, when the floodgates of communication, connection, content creation, and global scalability have been opened wide.

When it's fun, it flows. And when it flows, it grows. This principle applies to life and especially social media.

Be.
timeless

Social media is fast, fleeting, and ephemeral.
The aim in building a personal brand is to be
timeless. The greatest thought leaders
transcend the ever-changing landscape
of social media. Be the next great one.
Transcend.

We've all just gotta be, 'cause
answers rarely come easily.
We've all just gotta be, then
finally, finally we're <u>free.</u>

Basement Jaxx

PART 3: BE. FREE

CHAPTER 17

EVERYTHING IS ENERGY

"If you have control over how
people interpret you, why not use it?"

You could completely ditch everything you've learned in this book so far. You could burn up your Personal Brand Hologram, forgo publishing a single iota of Pinnacle Content, never send out a pitch email, and shut down all of your social media accounts. In fact, you could do your very best to obliterate your entire online presence, and you could very well succeed.

Guess what?

You *still* have a personal brand.

Now, I'm not recommending you do any of the above. The internet provides an unparalleled ability to scale your brand (and thus your business) in an unprecedented capacity, and I can safely assume that's why you're here in the first place. But for the purposes of hypothesis, say you *were* considering going incognito for a minute. Say you were downright exhausted from keeping up with the ever-increasing demand of being "known." Say you felt depleted from the constant expectation to be present, recent, and relevant in today's digital world. (I certainly can relate!) Say you just wanted to, you know, lay low.

Sorry to be the bearer of bad news, but your personal brand is still alive and well. Unlike your smartphone, it's not something you can turn on and off. Your brand exists purely based on the fact that you interface with *other human beings* every single day. Like, in the real world. Whether that be your employees, your clients, your boss, your friends, your network—or perhaps your barista or bus driver—you are always on some version of a stage, and everyone is some version of your audience. Based on the way you carry yourself, how you engage, and how you treat people, you are thereby constantly telling a story, leaving an impression, and imparting a memory upon everyone you meet.

This is branding.

Most people are completely unaware of how they are "showing up." You are *living* your brand, every single second of every single day, and have the ability to impact your business with the vibration of energy that you bring to it. And *everything* is a living form of vibration. Or more plainly stated: everything is energy.

This isn't woo-woo. This is actually science. As Albert Einstein said, "Everything is energy and that's all there is to it. Match the frequency of the reality you want, and you cannot help but get that reality. There can be no other way. This is not philosophy. This is physics."

Quantum physics to be exact.

What quantum physics essentially proves is that there is nothing solid in the universe, because everything in the universe is composed of atoms. As some of us might remember from middle school science class, atoms contain three different subatomic particles inside them: protons, neutrons, and electrons. The protons and neutrons are packed together into the center of the atom, while the electrons whiz around the outside. The electrons move so quickly that we never know exactly where they are from one moment to the next. In reality, atoms that form objects we consider solid are actually made up of 99.99999 percent space.

And, as everything is made of atoms, this shows us that everything is made up of energy. This book is energy. The coffee cup you're sipping from is energy. The clothes you're wearing are energy. Guess what else is also energy? I am. So are you. And perhaps, the most potent, electric and important form of energy is the space in *between* me and you.

Becoming aware of the power of energy means becoming aware of the power of *your* energy. Harnessing that energy becomes a professional competitive advantage. Mastering it becomes a superpower.

AN AWKWARD AMAZING FIRST IMPRESSION

One of the most important people in my life also happens to be one of the most important people at SimplyBe: Aleksa Narbutaitis, the first person I ever hired. Hiring Aleksa helped me to scale my business to where it is today. Of all the moments she and I have shared over the years, one of the most memorable is the day she came in to interview for an assistant position.

In true Aleksa form, she showed up twenty minutes early. The receptionist had walked her back to my office, unaware I was in the middle of finishing up a phone call with a huge client. The receptionist, and subsequently Aleksa, barreled into my office unannounced. Holding my hand over my phone, I politely asked Aleksa to head back to reception, letting her know I would come get her momentarily.

I will never forget how grounded, calm, and unfazed by the mix-up she seemed. In full transparency, I was the one who felt stressed. And yet, Aleksa—this stranger—said with a matching whisper and a genuine smile, "No problem," and gracefully headed out. My energy dramatically shifted. I instantly felt soothed. My tension all but disappeared. Suddenly, I found myself extremely eager to finish my phone call so that I could go meet this young woman.

To be frank, the only thing I specifically remember about our first meeting is that awkward moment before the interview had actually started and how gracefully she handled it. In a split second, with barely any words spoken, Aleksa told a full story about herself, and I intuitively knew two things: she would remain calm under pressure (a huge asset in a growing start-up like mine) and she would be easy to be around (a huge bonus to have as an assistant working in a small company in close proximity to one another day in and day out). Did her resume, credentials, and referrals also help her win the job? Of course. Did I need to look at Aleksa's digital presence to learn she could and would be amazing to work with? Actually . . . no. It was her energy that told that story. It was her energy that guaranteed her the job as my assistant. Today, she's our creative director and runs SimplyBe.'s entire creative department.

I want you to think about the people in your life who have positively impacted your career the most. These can be your business partners, your best clients, your all-star employees, your inspiring mentors, or your favorite bosses. Think about the time you first met them. Maybe you remember where you were or what you both wore. Most likely you remember the key things you said that shaped your perspective on who they would be in your life and who you could be to them. But I bet what you remember most about those first meetings is how you *felt* in those moments. Perhaps they were feelings of excitement, passion, empowerment, safety, or a sense of trust. Ask yourself what it was precisely about them that made you feel this way? Was it their smile, their handshake, the way they sat, their body language, or their tone of voice? These nuances are the energetic data points that imprint someone's "brand" into our minds and hearts.

On the flip side, think about the people you have crossed paths with who didn't end up being the best people to work with. Maybe you identified that "off" feeling right away, or you ended up working with them nonetheless, only for it to eventually turn south. This is intuition, and we all have moments where we ignore it. (It's all divine; it's how we learn.) But our intuition is never wrong, and it all comes down to the energy we experience. If you were to go back to these meetings and pinpoint the emotions you experienced in these initial interactions, could you name them now? How did you feel?

You have the same exact ability to make an impression (or rather, *design* an impression) as all the people who have ever made an impression on you.

And *impression* is just another word for "brand," my friend.

Your brand is expressed in everything you do and everything you are. From the way you dress, to the way you walk into a room, to the way you make eye contact, to the way you stand, to the way you talk, to the way you decorate your desk, it all tells a story.

It's simply about becoming conscious.

CHOOSE YOUR VIBE

I can be moody as hell. I am also a closet introvert and get my energy from solitude. But the truth is, I have to show up most days and be "on" in front of a lot of people all the time, whether they are my team, my clients, or hundreds of people at a speaking engagement. There have been countless moments where I would rather be chilling on my couch in yoga pants with a pint of coconut ice cream and my dogs, whose company I often prefer over that of people.

One of those moments happened not too long ago, on a day that I was scheduled for a speaking engagement for three hundred people at a real estate conference. That morning, I woke up feeling like shit. I was leaving for a big trip a few days later and hadn't slept in weeks due to the anxiety. As a result, my throat was swollen, and my head was congested. I so, *so* badly wanted to bail. I was filled with resentment that I couldn't. My inner bitch was raging.

In the Uber ride over, I made a *conscious* choice to shift. I wasn't only going to crush it onstage, I was going to walk into the venue and greet everyone with grace, gratitude, and light. I made a point to shake hands and smile into the eyes of everyone I met. I profusely said "thank you" to the client for the lovely setup they bestowed on me as a speaker. Most importantly, I gave my talk with full presence, positivity, and passion. And when I left, I hugged the stage manager, the owner of the company, and of course, the client who booked me, goodbye. Not only did it end up being one of the best talks of my career to date, the client circled back to me less than two weeks later inviting me to speak at their annual national conference for a thousand plus people in Las Vegas.

Imagine if I had let my inner bitch get the best of me that day? Imagine if I had treated the gig like a mandatory job versus a humbling opportunity? Imagine if I had let my bad vibes lead and showed up with the attitude of, "Fuck it, this is me today. Deal with it."

Choose your vibes and change the course of your life.

SPEAK UP

Last year, I was leading a public speaking training for the team at SimplyBe., most of which are young women in their twenties. As a core value as CEO, I am fiercely committed to investing in their personal and professional development. Given that the entire team interacts with clients all day every day, particularly in client presentations, it was essential that I train them on how to speak more confidently in front of our external partners. I had given them an assignment to put together a ten-minute presentation of their choice and bring it to the team training. Each of them would get up, one at a time, and present their slides to the entire group. I would record them so they could watch themselves after the meeting for further self-study. I'll never forget my dear employee Mary's presentation. It's important here to note that in everyday life, Mary speaks with gravity in her voice, has extreme conviction in her personal opinions (sometimes bordering on sassy), and has a boisterous belly laugh.

Mary had put together a beautiful presentation on the top five principles she had learned about self-growth at SimplyBe., something that she had taken upon herself to develop without my direction or request. I was not only touched by this but immediately impressed. This was above and beyond expectations.

She walked up to the front of the room, hooked up her laptop to the monitor, and cleared her throat. As soon as she opened her mouth to speak, a voice came out that didn't sound like Mary at all. It was high-pitched and airy, almost like a whisper. Her voice was shaky and seemed to be coming from her head, not from her chest, let alone her belly. She sounded younger than she actually was. Instantly, she lost her credibility.

It was painfully evident how nervous she was and clear that she did not trust herself. All of this stemmed from the simple act of *how* she used her voice. Her fantastic presentation slides didn't make any difference. None of us were paying attention to them because her nervousness was all we could fixate on. Had Mary shared her presentation using her *actual* voice, usually filled with confidence, personality, and gravity, it would have been a very different presentation. Mary would have presented a very different personal brand story.

You probably can relate to Mary's experience. It's nerve-racking to speak publicly for most people, and the truth is, building a personal brand will require you to speak in front of people at one point or another. Now, there's no need to panic and run to the nearest vocal coach or sign up for the next speaker training. There are a few essential best practices and key hacks to harness your personal brand voice.

For starters, understand where your voice is "coming from." Let's do an experiment and practice introducing yourself. Let's start with a body scan. Close your eyes and start to become aware of the following parts of your physical body: the top of your head, moving down to your throat, then to your chest, then to your belly, then to your groin, and finally to the bottoms of your feet. Become "aware" of these parts by visualizing that part of your body, acknowledging it, and taking one breath, in and out, at each point.

Once you have gone through the body scan, open your eyes and *from your head* say, "Hi, my name is_____. It's nice to meet you." Then continue moving down your body saying the same phrase from your throat, then your chest, your belly, your groin, and finally, your feet.

What differences did you notice? Perhaps when you spoke from your feet, you felt grounded. Clearly, you're not speaking out of your feet here, but the sensation of feeling your feet on the ground while you speak creates an experience of groundedness, and you therefore technically *sound* different. Perhaps when you spoke from your groin, you felt more alive. When you speak from your groin, you omit a sense of power, as you're connecting to one of the largest energetic sources of creation in your body. What did you feel when you spoke from your chest? Perhaps you felt a tinge of emotions, as when you speak from that point, you're literally communicating from your heart center. When you spoke from your head, you most likely felt—well—*in your head*. And we all know that "being in our head" is generally a result of overthinking, which takes us out of the moment and impacts our ability to be present. And being present is a key component to speaking in front of anyone with confidence, conviction, and clarity.

Secondly, hit your consonants. This might sound silly but don't underestimate the power of articulation. PUNCH your Ps, BOOM your Bs, TICK your Ts, and KICK your Ks and watch how much clearer you come across. These little nuances not only communicate to your listener on a subconscious level that you're confident, they literally make you easier to understand. In other words: Clear articulation makes you stand out. It makes what you have to say memorable, and as such, it makes *you* memorable. It also suggests a level of sophistication, and where there is sophistication, there is an insinuation of experience, and where there is insinuation of experience, there is an inherent trust. A trust in YOU that you are someone not only to listen to but someone to know, to work with, and to invest in.

All this from the manner in which you say the word *possibility*, with a dash of *kindness*?

Yup.

Finally, just breathe. Your breath is your savior. Don't be afraid to speak slowly and take your sweet-ass time when you're speaking. Don't forget that it's you who's holding the floor. Reclaim your poise, one inhale and exhale at a time.

Everything is branding! Everything matters. Everything is energy. The best part? We all have the power of CHOICE. We get to choose how we live our brand, from how we stand, to how we speak, to how we smile, to how we shake hands, to how we project, to how we articulate our words. It's all messaging and it's ALL energy. And when we take control of our energy, we don't only take control of our experience that day.

We take control of our destiny.

Be.

electric

You are electric. Harness your energy and
leave a spark wherever you go. The space
between us is magic. This isn't woo-woo.
This is science.

CHAPTER 18

COLOR YOUR LIFE

"Fashion is not something that exists
in dresses only. Fashion exists in the sky,
in the street. Fashion has to do with ideas,
the way we live, what is happening."

Coco Chanel

It was the summer of 2016. Ryan Lochte was making a muck of the Rio Olympics, people were falling off cliffs chasing Pokémon, LeBron James had led the Cleveland Cavaliers in a Game 7 victory against the Golden State Warriors, 93 to 89, and Snapchat had become all the rage.

And, on one particular Sunday, I was sitting on an airplane. It was actually the Sunday night of that unforgettable Game 7. I was on my way down to my corporate job in Dallas. And I was *pissed at life*. Partially because I hated that corporate job but mainly because all my friends were watching LeBron James's epic comeback at a sports bar, while I was stuck on an O'Hare tarmac instead. It's important to note that I am *not* a sports fan by any stretch of the imagination. I am, however, an occasional victim of FOMO. Moral of the story: I wanted to be anywhere to watch that game but on that airplane.

Not letting my self-pity get the best of me, I whipped out my iPhone and opened up my Safari app and typed in www.espn.com. I figured they would have live video coverage of the game, and I was surprisingly right. However, the damn video wouldn't load. Ever more frustrated, I closed out Safari and popped open Snapchat. Up until that day, I had barely used it, thinking it was a ridiculous waste of time only teenagers could appreciate. (Read: I didn't understand how to use it.) But I did vaguely recall there being something called a "Discovery Channel" inside the app, where news media channels of all types streamed content. "Maybe ESPN has a Snap channel," I thought to myself. Turns out, my intuition led me to a basketball game that not only changed my life but also the future of my brand style.

You see, as I sat there on American Airlines flight #1322 from Chicago to Dallas, I was transported in real time to courtside seats in Cleveland, Ohio. I watched the entire final five minutes of Game 7 in ten-second video increments taken by fans who were sitting so close to the actual event, I could see LeBron's sweat on my tiny phone screen. I didn't need to spend thousands of dollars to sit where they were sitting. I *was* sitting there, feeling the energy of the crowd and the intensity of the players and witnessing my own heart beat with the kind of anxiety only a point-for-point live sporting event can give you.

At that moment, I had an epiphany. Snapchat was not a social media channel. It was a real-time window into the world. It was going to revolutionize the way in which we created and consumed content forever. I decided then and there that I was going to learn everything there was to know about this app and become the *Snapchat expert*.

And so, I "became about it." I blogged about it, I vlogged about it, I talked about it, and even put my Snapcode on my business card. Shortly thereafter, I became recognized as a "Snapchat expert" by the *Chicago Tribune* and a series of top podcasts. (A testament to the power of creating content consistently and constantly to build authority.) This was the same exact time I was scheming to quit that corporate gig and launch SimplyBe. I had invested in a visual brand style guide to develop my logo, fonts, colors, and icons. Of course, I incorporated Snapchat's sunny yellow, as it was my biggest inspiration at the time, and I actually had plans to make SimplyBe. Agency Snapchat-focused.

This turned out to be one of the happiest accidents of my career. You see, my Snapchat obsession faded, but the color yellow stuck. (I use Insta Stories exclusively now, another artifact of the fleeting nature of social media. But I digress.) Today, yellow has become so much more than a color. It's become the essence of my entire brand. To me, yellow represents joy, confidence, boldness, authenticity, fun, sunshine, and light. These are all things that I want the story of SimplyBe. to embody, as well as me, Jessica, the face of the brand.

Yellow comes to life on my website and on social media channels. It's still alive and well on my business cards. You will find the color yellow generously but tastefully integrated into SimplyBe.'s office decor. I often receive yellow gifts from clients and friends. The color yellow takes up half of my closet. Over the course of the last few years, I have amassed a collection of bags, shoes, blazers, and dresses in my favorite hue.

This all might seem trite, or cute at best, but the color yellow has officially, positively, and hugely impacted my career. Read: I have received unparalleled exposure by the sheer consistency and therefore memorability of this color. I get recognized by the media, by influencers I bring onto my podcast, by clients I want to work with, and by my online community due to the unforgettable nature of yellow, and my boldness in using it. You've probably noticed how half of this book is dripping in it. My confidence in this color choice is a reflection of my self-worth and has a direct correlation to my net worth.

This is no accident. This is branding.

It's all been intentionally architected to trigger you to have an emotional response to my brand, and most importantly, to *remember* it.

You have the power to do the same.

A HOODIE AND A PANTSUIT WALK INTO SOHO HOUSE

We are visual creatures. That's why your style, not your voice or even your energy, is the final piece to craft when it comes to living your brand. Speaking of energy, most people are walking through the world unconscious of their own, let alone able to fully receive yours. That's why perhaps the most important component to living your brand is getting clear on your personal brand style, as it's something tangible people can easily remember you by.

Fun fact: we process visual information sixty thousand times faster than written or verbal information. In other words, style makes not only a lasting but a fast impression. Remember, impression = brand, and the world we live in is becoming increasingly saturated and fast-paced, so you have to find ways to immediately stand out.

Style is important for this reason, but also because your style defines who you are, whether you realize it or not. Style is how you announce yourself to the world. It's how you show up for that next meeting, on-line webinar, or event. Whether it's your signature bright lipstick, your amazing shoes, your cool pair of glasses, or your casual vibe, you have something that is your "signature"—even if you don't know it yet.

Let me be clear about something. Having a strong sense of style is not the same as having a great sense of fashion. I am not encouraging you to run to the store and pick up the latest edition of *Vogue*. You don't have to pay attention to a single "trend." I certainly don't. This part of your brand has nothing to do with being *fashionable*. It does, however-er, have everything to do with being *you*. It's about examining what's most likely already in your closet, or even currently on your body, and getting clear on why you might be wearing it, what you want it to say about you, and then owning it.

If you own your signature look as much as you own your mission, your growth, and your message, your aesthetic becomes synonymous with something deeper, and in turn, helps you stand out from the rest of the pack.

Let's take the signature look of high-heeled shoes, for example. Say you are a power female executive, and you are never seen without your high heels. You show up to meetings, get featured in the press, attend power lunches, and stand on stages to give keynote speeches all while wearing your signature heels. Over and over again, you wear them. With time, those heels begin to stand for something. They represent not just you and your message, but badass, powerful, executive women everywhere. When people see another female executive in high heels, they're reminded of you.

This might seem extreme (I personally can't stand wearing heels, but I do love me a kitten heel bootie), but the point is that your consistency in your look becomes signature to your personal brand, and that signature style can be leveraged to make you memorable. And memorability = branding.

It's essential to figure out what you love about your own style and how you can use it to spread the message and awareness of your personal brand. Now, it's easy to think that hyperfocusing on what you wear and how you show up is the opposite of freedom. The aim here is not to stress about it but rather to free yourself to *own* your unique style. This is *living your brand*.

Let's take a look at some well-known personal brands and examine how their signature styles have not only defined their careers but their industries, communities, political endeavors, and in many ways, the world. Yep—clothing and the authenticity behind it can be *that* powerful. So can yours.

Mark Zuckerberg's Hoodie

When Mark Zuckerberg founded Facebook, it wasn't so much his insistence on remaining the CEO of a multimillion-dollar company at the age of twenty-four that shocked the public. It was that he continued to wear a hoodie. In a single decision to wear what he wanted, he inadvertently inspired tech start-up founders everywhere and unconsciously created an aspirational lifestyle in Silicon Valley (and beyond).

This was a lifestyle where you could disrupt industries, make millions, and wear whatever the fuck you wanted along the way. Roll your eyes if you wish, but Zuckerberg's hoodie has received more media than most people do. It's been featured extensively in the *Washington Post*, *GQ*, the *Atlantic*, the *Guardian*, the *Wall Street Journal* and on CNN to name a few. Some called his hoodie donning a "mark of immaturity" while others interpreted it as an expression of originality and individuality.[1] I believe that the hoodie, in the context of male tech entrepreneurs, symbolizes the desire to be in control of your own destiny. We can all make our own assessment from this stretch of cotton and stitching, but like it or not, the hoodie has nonetheless become one of the most iconic style choices of the millennial generation. No matter how you personally might feel about him, there is no one else to give credit to for that more than Mark Zuckerberg.

Hillary Clinton's Pantsuit

Neither Republicans nor Democrats can deny the strategic power of former US secretary of state and presidential nominee Hillary Clinton's pantsuit. In fact, it's safe to say the pantsuit itself has become practically *synonymous* with the name Hillary Clinton. Women publicly wearing pants have had a political and social charge since the last century, and Hillary Clinton's choice was by no means accidental.

While many of her first lady predecessors were known for their gowns and skirts, Clinton rocked the pantsuit as an outward sign of her ambition to level the playing field for men and women. She went to great pains to distinguish herself from other first ladies, emphasizing her own career, causes, and passions rather than simply her role in relation to her husband.[2] Her penchant for pantsuits has become so well-known it has spawned memes, *Saturday Night Live* sketches, and Halloween costumes. Not least of all, it inspired a viral hashtag and the creation of a three-million-member-strong Facebook fan page, aptly titled #PantsuitNation. The group's founder, Libby Chamberlain, told BBC that "the pantsuit is the symbol of women's fight for equality in the workplace."[3] Even the different colors she wore carried their own innuendos.

When Hillary Clinton accepted her nomination for president at the Democratic National Convention, she wore white, the color worn by suffragettes. When she delivered her concession speech after her defeat by President Trump, she wore a Ralph Lauren pantsuit in purple. Purple is the color of bipartisanship, as blue and red mixed together make purple. It was said that this was a subtle call for unity, which echoed sentiments from her speech: "We have seen that our nation is more deeply divided than we thought," she said. "But I still believe in America, and I always will."[4]

Hillary Clinton's personal brand messaging probably could have used some work in the 2016 election, but her pantsuit (and the impact it's had in the media, on her supporters, and on society at large) is one of the most exemplary acts of signature style that I have ever seen.

Chance the Rapper's #3 Baseball Hat

A few years ago, I saw Chance the Rapper at Soho House in Chicago. Given I am an obsessive Chance fan, I almost had a heart attack. There he was, a mere ten feet away from me, playing pool with his buddies, laughing and sporting his signature #3 baseball hat. At Soho House, it's a member code (and a legitimate policy) to leave celebrities alone. I perspired in the corner as I texted all my friends: "OMG, YOU GUYS. CHANCE. AT SOHO. OMG." (Subtle, I know.) Flash forward to a few weeks later. I was back at Soho House, sipping an oat milk latte, when a guy who kind of looked like Chance caught my attention. While it *wasn't* Chance the Rapper, he was sporting Chance's same #3 hat. In an instant, I felt my heart literally warm with the thought, "I don't know that guy . . . but I *like* that guy." I didn't need to actually know this stranger across the way to understand that we had something very deep in common: our love for the same artist.

Not only is Chance a talented musician, he represents Chicago—my hometown. He represents action against gun violence—a cause close to my heart. He is an advocate for Chicago public school students and teachers alike—my mom was an inner-city high school teacher for thirty-five years. Chance loves God; so do I. As I looked at this stranger, it dawned on me: signature style doesn't only express your brand, it unites your people. It cultivates community without you even needing to be present. A signature style, especially when it is associated with a mission-driven brand message like Chance's, has the power to connect people who are otherwise strangers and transforms them into potential allies and even friends. This is the true power of signature style.

And to me, yellow isn't just a style. It's sunshine reflecting off the Chicago river. It's the chairs in the lobby of my office. It's my favorite coat, which I wear every winter even when it's just a little too cold to do so. It's the experience of bright light filling the depths of my heart with joy. And I would like to believe that when a stranger sees the color yellow, they experience that too . . . and think of me.

WHAT'S YOUR SIGNATURE STYLE?

Open up your closet, peruse your social media photos, and consider what you LOVE to wear the most. Then take the worksheet below to drill down into your own signature style, and above all, where and how you can leverage it to make your personal brand that much more memorable. And when you're done, go out and live it.

Owning—and honing—what makes you feel you, then rocking it consistently, constantly, and with unapologetic authenticity is the making of a strong, signature personal brand style. For me, it's the color yellow. What is it for you?

ROCK YOUR LOOK

What does style mean to you?

Name three people whose style you admire and why:

What five words define your personal style now?

What five words do you want to define your personal style?

Ask your family and friends how they would define your style.

What's your favorite piece of clothing or accessory and why?

What is your signature piece of clothing, makeup, or accessory?

Based on your answers above, write out your signature style mission statement, for example, *"I rock the color yellow because it's bright as the fucking sun and so am I."*

Be.
signature

What you wear tells a story. Understanding
this is a superpower. Tell your story by
rocking what makes you feel good.
Nothing exudes confidence and
memorability like a signature style.

CHAPTER 19

THE FUTURE OF BUSINESS IS . . .

"A boss has the title. A leader has the people."

Simon Sinek

My first introduction to corporate America was a rude awakening.

In between Cheeky and SimplyBe. Agency, I took a transition job working for a five-hundred-person travel company for a hot minute. (Actually, it was two years.) My job was to innovate a new private dining and entertainment membership across twenty-five international markets. As a result, I had the great fortune of jet-setting to over fifteen countries, meeting people from different cultures while I built infrastructures, strategies, and teams on a global scale. During this time, my depth of experience expanded tremendously, as I developed a business acumen I had never had before as a new entrepreneur.

Yet I learned another side of business during these years too. For starters, I quickly noticed how no one at this company seemed to actually *enjoy* their job. At first, I didn't understand. Wasn't this supposed to be a "fun" place to work? We were innovating every day. We had perks

GALORE. It was a travel company! Who doesn't love travel? Yet over the course of my time there, it became blatantly clear why there was such a gap.

Everywhere you turned, there was red tape. There was an unmistakable hierarchy that made anyone who wasn't in the C-suite feel small and replaceable. As a result, gossip ran rampant, and employees across the board operated from a place of scarcity. Practically everyone felt afraid to speak up in meetings, push back on their manager, or present original ideas to their teams. It was a "me versus you" environment, and it became abundantly clear just how toxic it was.

As a company, you can have the most beautiful, exciting product in the world. You can have the best process and the tightest systems in the game. You can have enviable perks and work in an exciting industry. You can even have a brilliant vision to change the world. But if the people who work for you hate their jobs, your organization ultimately won't succeed.

When I took a closer look at the true "why" behind the clearly broken environment I was working within, I didn't have to look far. I just had to look *up*. I happened to be on a senior-level team that had constant exposure to the founder of the company. He was no doubt an unforgettable personality. When he walked into the room, everyone could *feel it*. His energy was powerful, and his voice was deep and distinct. He had a big, bold, and worldly vision. In truth, it was hard not to *want* to believe in him. He was infectious, capturing the attention of the room (and the whole organization) like a master. His influence over the company was palpable. His power was undeniable.

But, there was just one small problem: everyone was terrified of him.

The way he engaged with his staff was dominating and insincere. Every directive he gave was a command, not a conversation. He spoke over people in meetings, often slamming his hands on the table to make his points, causing the room to paralyze. It became abundantly clear that the objective of every project we worked on was to "make him happy," versus what was best for our customers. We all quietly knew we had been hired to drive profit, not purpose. This was felt by everyone, from the senior staff like me, all the way down to the entry-level workers, causing a ripple effect of fear and ultimately, resentment.

Just a few months after I left that job, I got the news that the company had to downsize, with multimillions in lost revenue. Hundreds of people lost their jobs.

My story is by no means unique. It's a microcosmic case study in the universe of toxic workplaces. For this to become the exception, not the rule, however, change must start with the leaders of these organizations. Regardless of the size of your employee base, industry, or gross revenue, if you lead, you need to take a long, hard look at how you "show up." You need to understand your personal brand.

Legendary management consultant and writer Peter Drucker once said, "Culture eats strategy for breakfast." Culture is how you treat people. It's the tone you set based upon how *human* you are willing to be with your people. The more human you are as a leader, the greater impact you can have. And isn't that impact the goal? Not just for the leader, but for every company, brand, board, and employee?

As CEO of SimplyBe., I know that I create impact every morning when I walk into my office. I can make a beeline for my desk, disconnected and filled with superiority, or I can make eye contact, smile, and say hello to my employees and ask them how they are doing. In meetings, I make space for their opinions and their ideas. At their reviews, I point out their strengths and talents, as well as their opportunities for growth.

None of this is actually complicated; nor does it require hours of my time. It simply comes down to treating people how you want to be treated. It's all a reflection of *my* brand as the face, founder, and leader of my organization. This is what ultimately drives success for my business.

This doesn't make me special or better than any other CEO out there. What it does make me, however, is conscious. Conscious leadership creates conscious culture. Conscious culture attracts conscious people, and conscious people form conscious teams.

And conscious leadership, cultures, and teams are the future of business.

SCALING THE FUTURE

Through my work as the leader of SimplyBe., I am exposed to a lot of different types of work environments. I am often hired to come in and lead discovery sessions, train a small team of people, teach a workshop to a department, or present a lunch and learn to an entire company. Whether it's for a burgeoning tech start-up of a dozen people or a corporate organization of thousands, one thing is always clear: *people are starving for humanity in business.*

Employees across the board are desperate to feel seen, uplifted, and inspired. They are dying to feel free to be *themselves* at work. What's more, they crave the *permission* to be themselves at work. In most cases, being fully authentic at work is the exception, not the rule. This saddens me.

It also gives me immense hope.

The space of personal branding doesn't only benefit your own unique career path. Having a personal brand is becoming an ever-increasing, universal business asset for all employees, teams, and leaders across all industries, and companies are indeed waking up to this. When an individual can clearly communicate their unique value and confidently "simply be" who they are every day at work, this becomes an organizational superpower. Imagine what would happen if every person inside a company had the clarity, the confidence, and the passion to become a true brand ambassador? That company's impact would be unparalleled.

What's more, when people feel that who they *are*—not just what they *do*—is valued, they become happier, more engaged, and more productive at work.

When an organization empowers its workforce to build their own brands, this not only unifies a clearly articulated company message, it also establishes a leverageable, digital presence that enhances credibility and external optics, while increasing internal collaboration, company pride, and a positive culture. To build a fully integrated, deeply authentic workforce is the secret sauce to scaling your business.

This requires an understanding of where "authenticity" actually comes to life in the workplace—and where it fails to do so. By this point, you probably feel completely aligned to your own fully authentic brand message. But where the rubber meets the road is when the people around you—primarily the people who work for you—feel confident to express their own authenticity too. Assuming you are building your brand to grow your business, and your business ultimately needs other people beside you to run it, you must unleash the personal brands of your people to support your business, understand it, and help it grow.

LOVE OVER FEAR: A LOOK AT LEADERSHIP

Leaders today all have a choice: to operate from a place of fear (which is expressed as ego) or from a place of love (which is expressed as service).

Think about a leader you know who is operating with his or her ego. Chances are they intimidate you. This can perpetuate an unhealthy sense of admiration at best or total resentment at worst. Now think of a leader who is leading with love. Chances are you like being in their orbit. They inspire you to believe in their mission. What's more, they inspire you to believe in yourself.

Whether you're a CEO running a thousand-person company or a solopreneur managing a personal assistant, now is the time in your personal branding journey to open your eyes to the power—and responsibility—you possess. It's time to take all this work you've done on yourself and apply it to the people you lead.

We get to decide to build our businesses with love or with fear. We get to choose whether or not our organizations will stand for something greater than our net profit.

It starts with our vision. It comes to life in our mission. It's upheld in our values.

We all have the power to be a magnetic, effective, and powerful leader. We get to decide what ripple effect we will create in the world.

BUT, NO ONE CAN CHANGE THE WORLD

A couple years ago, I was meeting with my new client Larry, a CEO of a large technology company. During our onboarding interview, as he was explaining his new artificial intelligence software, he boldly exclaimed, "Jessica, I want to change the world." Then he paused and said, "I take that back. I don't want to change the world. I can't change the world. No one can. But I want to change *my corner of it*. Imagine what the world would be if we all did?"

Therein lies the bedrock to not only successful organizations but a brighter future. Passionate, human, authentic, purpose-driven leaders who are willing to wear their missions (and their humility) on their sleeves.

We all have a responsibility to make the world a better place, but we cannot do it alone. It takes a village. If you're building a company in order to do so, you need to get your people behind you. And your people need to feel that they have a seat at the table as an influencer of change too.

This goes deeper than an open brainstorm in an innovation meeting. It's more than saying a quick "hello" to your staff as you walk into the office each day. This needs to be woven into the fabric of the organization at the deepest of levels. When you do this effectively, watch how your people come to work with a renewed spirit, energy, and attitude knowing that the work they are doing truly matters. To get to the bottom of how this materializes, let's revisit the idea of company values, or core values, to be exact.

Take a quick pulse check to ask yourself the following:

- *Does my company have core values?*
- *If so, what are they?*
- *Do my employees know what they are as well as I do?*
- *Most importantly, are we **living** our core values and are we keeping ourselves accountable for maintaining them?*

I was actually first presented with the idea of core values at my former corporate job. The idea of having a set of well-defined values, a "rally cry" if you will, deeply inspired me. It made me feel so good that my work in the world wasn't only intended to collect a paycheck for myself but to change the lives of others. I believe all human beings have a deep psychological, primal yearning for purpose and a desire to make a difference.

Sadly, this was yet another gaping hole I witnessed at that organization. Sure, they had core values, and they were beautifully plastered on the walls in expensive frames for all to see, but at the end of the day, they meant nothing. They were big, abstract statements that no one could explain, let alone embody. They were bullshit.

At SimplyBe., I made the decision to establish core values that not only meant something but that everyone could easily understand. Above all, I implemented structures and modalities for the organization to actually *live* the values day in and day out, over time.

Here are the SimplyBe. core values:

SIMPLYBE.'S CORE VALUES

BE. BOLD

We embrace our fears and constantly step outside our comfort zones, as we know that's the only way to truly grow.

BE. KIND

We don't work with assholes.

Period.

BE. RELEVANT

We study our industry with insatiable curiosity, in order to stay ahead of marketing and branding trends and remain a best-in-class company.

BE. TRUE

We celebrate showing up fully and authentically every day at work.

BE. IN SERVICE

We dedicate time to giving back to communities and organizations for social impact and goodwill.

BE. EXTRAORDINARY

We go above and beyond the call of duty, always striving for excellence in an effort to impress no one else but ourselves.

Theoretically, these are great. But in designing these values, I wanted to ensure they would not just become pretty notions that we stuck on the proverbial company wall. I knew as I wrote them, I couldn't change my corner of the world if I was the only one who knew them, loved them, and lived them.

To mitigate the potential for meaninglessness, I have put a simple mechanism in place at SimplyBe. called the Core Values Round Table. It's a biweekly thirty-minute meeting where the entire team identifies a specific example that they witnessed of each member of the team "living the values." The aim here is to identify tangible moments of action, versus embellishing emotions. As such, these core value specifics have to be "tweet" length.

We have had this meeting like clockwork over the past three years and as a result, the core values have become embedded in the ethos of SimplyBe. Every other week, we gather in a conference room around a table or on a Zoom call and one at a time, share our observations of each other. It goes something like this:

- *"Kristin, you were **bold** this month in leading your first client pitch. Your confidence shined at a new level."*
- *"Aleksa, thank you for suggesting the team take the course you found on TikTok for brands. This makes us increasingly **relevant** as an agency and is going to add even more value to our clients in the future."*
- *"Nora, your work with our client has been so **extraordinary** that they are re-upping their engagement with us for another twelve months. This is a direct result of the incredible relationship you have built with them as their account manager."*

To some, this might look like a meeting filled with compliments. And that is part of it. But in truth, these micro-actions have created a dedication among my staff that upholds our culture as well as the vision of my company. They know that the way they "show up" (i.e., their personal brands) matters to the success, the bottom line, and the impact we are making as an organization. They have true ownership. And as a result, we keep scaling.

Like Larry, I have a grand vision for SimplyBe. to change my corner of the world. All good leaders need to have such a vision. But in order for it to actually be effective, it has to be tangible to the people you've put in charge of helping you bring it to life. And when you can provide the actual micro-opportunities for your people to feel seen, valued, and connected as they build that vision along the way, the game changes. Your workforce changes. Your business changes. Your impact changes.

The world changes.

INSPIRER > SURVIVOR

True authenticity, as I have explained, comes down to "embracing your shit" and using it in the service of others. But not everyone is prepared to embrace their shit. And sometimes, it's your colleagues, superiors, and employees who are the most resistant. After all, we're at *work*. It's not the place to be, you know, *emotional*. We have been conditioned to believe that our "9-to-5 self" is not the same as our "5-to-9 self."

Fuck that.

Your personal brand is not separate from your professional brand. They are one and the same. It is in the act of bringing your whole self to work (yes, with all of your "shit") that authenticity comes to life. This is nonetheless terrifying for most people. To be emotional and vulnerable at work means bringing down the shields that keep us safely protected behind our 9-to-5 armor. For many people, it is those very shields that have helped them to climb the rungs of the corporate ladder. Many professional people have great pride and attachment to their shields. To have "made it" takes a level of detachment and is a sign of admirable strength. Why would anyone want to take their shields down?

Let me tell you a story.

A few years back, I was invited to teach a two-day personal branding workshop for a ten-person executive marketing team at a Fortune 500 company. In preparation for the workshop, I had taken a prep call with the client, the director of the team, who debriefed me about each of his team members. He had specifically warned me about Sara. He explained that, while she was extremely talented, Sara was having a really hard time collaborating with the team as a whole. She was described as "defensive," "tough," and a "loner." She was on track to get a potential promotion, one that she really wanted, but my client made it clear she needed to work on her blind spots before any changes were made. The objective of all my workshops is not only to establish personal brand messaging but to invoke self-awareness in order for the group to identify what their message is in the first place. I knew I had my work cut out for me.

As the team entered the room, I could immediately point out Sara. She was exactly as described. We opened up the morning with a few icebreakers, a "Personal Branding 101" discussion, and a look at powerful case studies of personal brands in corporate America. By the afternoon, it was time for the group to build out their own Holograms. I had given the group time for a breakout session, and I noticed Sara was passionately, determinedly engaged in the exercise, head down, scribbling away. She had sticky notes spread out all over her station. I walked over, sat down beside her, and asked if she could show me what she was coming up with.

She swooped together her notes and proudly laid them out in front of me. "I am struggling to find the exact Headline, but I definitely think it's one of these," she said. Written on the sticky notes were the words *Survivor*, *Warrior*, and *Fighter*. I asked her to explain her rationale in coming up with these.

Sara responded, "No one understands what I have been through. I've always had to take care of myself. My mom didn't take care of me. I have paid my own way since I was young. I put myself through college, and I have moved across the country multiple times by myself. The only reason I have this job is because I've worked my ass off. No one has ever helped me get to where I am. I have done it all myself. So, I have had no choice but to be a fighter. No one understands what it's like to have to be a warrior in your own life. That's why I am a survivor."

I smiled and politely asked if I could use Sara's pen, to which she agreed. Slowly, I began to cross out the words *Survivor*, *Warrior*, and *Fighter*.

I looked her square in her eyes and said, "Based on what you just shared with me, Sara, what if you were *this* instead?" Next to the crossed-out words, I wrote the word *Inspiration*.

Within a second, Sara burst into such severe, hysterical tears, she had to leave the room. The simple act of reframing a few words on a note meant reframing the story of herself she had clung to her whole life. It meant removing the armor. It meant letting go of an entire identity and finding a new one.

By the end of our two days together, Sara was a different person. She was open, softer, engaged, and vulnerable. She even seemed more joyful. A few months later, I got the news from my client that Sara's performance at work had profoundly improved. She was communicating with more ease with internal team members, collaborating more effortlessly with external vendors, and was actually fun to be around at the office.

One year later, Sara reached out to me via email asking me for my home address. Within a week, I received a card in the mail from her with the news she had received that promotion and was once again moving across the country for it. She ended her note by saying, "Thank you for changing my life."

But I didn't change her life. She did. She chose to embrace her shit. She made the choice to take down the shield. She chose to rewrite the narrative from "Survivor" to "Inspiration." It was that single decision that changed the trajectory not only of Sara's career but her whole life.

Take an honest look at how *you* are showing up at work. Examine the self-talk you have ruminating in your head when you ponder your job. What's the lens you're looking through? What story do you keep telling yourself about yourself? What would happen to your relationships, your output, and most of all, your own experience of your job if you were to change that story? What would happen if you let down your shield?

Your shield is not your superpower.

Your truth is.

Lead with it.

IT STARTS WITH YOU

When I close my eyes and dream about the future of business, I see offices, meeting spaces, coworking hubs, presentation rooms, and networking events overflowing with one abundantly clear and unmistakable energy: our humanity. Despite your title, rank, or salary, remember we are all just people. Every single person you interact with at work is the same as you. They *are* you. Everyone experiences love, fear, pain, joy, triumph, and failure. It is our sheer humanity that beautifully binds us together. The day we bring this awareness to our work will be the day that the planet shifts. This might seem lofty, but it is the corporate organizations, public establishments, and private businesses that are, in fact, running the world.

The shift starts with one person at a time. It starts with leading from love instead of fear. It starts with having a vision and a mission more important than your net profit. It starts with knowing your values and taking a stand on them. It starts with giving your teams the space to know themselves, share themselves, and be themselves. It starts with believing that your power at work is found in your fully expressed multidimensional truth, not your two-dimensional persona.

It starts with you.

What kind of inspiration will you be?

THE FUTURE OF BUSINESS
STARTS WITH ME

When I lead from Love at work, I act like this:

When I lead from Fear at work, I act like this:

My vision for my company/business/brand/department/product is:

This is how I communicate my vision to my team or the people I work with:

Here are some examples of how I keep my "shield" up at work:

If I showed up as my true self at work, this is my biggest fear:

If I showed up as my true self at work, this is my biggest hope:

How can I take the work I have done thus far (my Hologram®, Supernova™, Pinnacle Content™, Orion's Star™ or Social Media plan) and use it to show up at work in a new way?

Be.

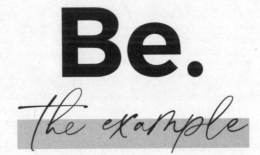

Any person with a platform has the
opportunity to inspire others. Know that no
audience or business is too small. You have
an obligation to set yourself free, and in
turn, you give everyone else around you
permission to do the same.

CHAPTER 20

FREEDOM REDEFINED

"Freedom is the oxygen of the soul."

Moshe Dayan

My relationship with the internet started in 1997, when at the wee age of sixteen, I signed up for my very own AOL Instant Messenger account. I would chat for hours on end with my friends, dissecting the latest hallway dramas of high school, gushing about my latest crush, or bitching about my parents. However, what I oddly recall the most specifically about my "IM" experience was not the conversations I had but ironically the password I chose when I set up my account. My username was Jezabell6. (A play on my initials and my favorite number, FYI.) And my password was "freedom."

For as long as I can remember, I have always been obsessed with the idea of freedom. Freedom has always felt romantic. Exhilarating. Seductive. Inspiring. Necessary. Even though I couldn't articulate it at that time, it's clear that freedom has been the consistent, number one core value of my life. When I was sixteen years young, I couldn't tell you exactly *why* I chose that as my password, but I do recall how *right* it felt.

It still does.

As I have evolved as a human being, a woman, and a professional, so has my relationship to the concept of freedom. As a rebellious teenager, freedom meant breaking the chains of my parents' seemingly insensible rules of curfews, good grades, and their no-dating-college-boys policy. At times, it meant blasting my music as loud as I wanted to in my room decorated with magazine clippings of my favorite bad boys like Christian Slater and Keanu Reeves. At other times, it meant flat-out running away. Which I actually did. Twice.

In my twenties, freedom meant doing *what* I wanted, *when* I wanted, with *whom* I wanted. This usually looked like hopping on a plane at a moment's notice to travel with my girlfriends, dating inappropriate but oh-so-sexy men (usually to my father's dismay), and trying out a multitude of day jobs, side hustles, and career paths until I settled on entrepreneurship.

Today, after nearly four decades here on this planet, my definition of freedom is, well, rather basic: it means simply being who I want to be.

This looks like living a life on my own terms, without the fear of judgment from other people. Period. Sure, there might be a bit of a rebellious undertone to my concept of freedom still. But now that I have a business, a brand, and a platform, I know that simply being me is more than a personal privilege; it's my obligation to the world.

At SimplyBe. Agency, our mission statement is this: "When you set yourself free to simply be, you set the world free."

As someone who holds the attention of others (i.e., your audience, your organization, and your community, no matter how big or small), your own expression of freedom can be a guiding light for others on the path to their own authentic expression. And, as I am sure you can relate to, finding yourself, knowing yourself, and being yourself isn't always easy. At times it can be downright dark. That's certainly been my experience.

When I look back at my darkest years filled with shit (before I learned how to embrace it), I vividly remember it was *other people* who inspired me to shift my perspective by showing me what was possible. It was in watching them that I began to redefine my definition of freedom. Sometimes they were people I knew personally—friends who had quit their joyless jobs to travel the world, left their unhappy marriages, come out of the closet, adopted a child on their own, started their own companies, shut down their companies, reinvented themselves, learned how to let things roll off, spoken truth to power, or given it all up for love. Many times, however, the people who shifted my perspective on freedom the most were those I didn't know personally at all. They were thought leaders, experts, and influencers whose books I had read, or whom I had watched on TV or followed on social media. My virtual mentors. People like Danielle LaPorte, Glennon Doyle, Maya Angelou, Gary Vaynerchuk, Lizzo, Brené Brown, Michael Jordan, and Lady Gaga. These people changed my life by simply being them. They showed me that I could simply be me too.

You are one of these people. Do not underestimate the power of your own platform, despite the size of its footprint. As we learned in the last chapter, no one person can change the world, but we *can* change our own corner of it. We change the world one person at a time. Simply be, and you create a domino effect of awakening.

Freedom does not reside on the internet, however, or on social media. You can't find it in the four walls of your office. And to be frank, it doesn't merely live in the lives of your brave friends, motivational speakers, and your favorite thought leaders. You can't sit on the sidelines and expect to experience true freedom.

Freedom lives within the deepest depths of your very own heart. It exists in the vast wide open landscape of your soul. It IS your soul. It's time you seek to understand it. It's time to dive as deep as you possibly can to know yourself, to know life, and to know the world. Therein lies your freedom. And therein lives your actual, authentic personal brand.

The one that the world needs.

Great personal brands cannot be great unless they experience their own lives to the fullest. They can't be inspirational if they themselves aren't being inspired. You find your material not in a book but out there in the vast wide open. You find your message not in a framework but in magical moments born from real-life experiences.

The most effective personal brands are the most infectious people, so go into the edges of your life and learn what lights you up. Then come back to this work.

Because even though we're wrapping up our time together, this isn't the end. It's the beginning.

Be.
free

It is our birthright to live a life that feels good
to us. You can't find this behind your desk, but
in the vast wide open edges of your life.
The real magic comes when you journey
there, in some way, every single day.
You deserve to live free.

CHAPTER 21

BE YOUR OWN HERO

"The warrior <u>knows</u> that her
heartbreak is her map."

Glennon Doyle

"Living free" is a sexy concept. But the truth is, the act of true freedom takes an immense amount of courage, as it means you have to step outside of that oh-so-familiar yet extremely dangerous abode: *your comfort zone.*

When we step outside of our comfort zones, we risk being wrong, disliked, rejected, damned, misunderstood, or exposed. This is the price we *all* pay on the path to authenticity.

And yet, no one changed the world by staying comfortable. Comfort zones are the enemy of freedom: your own *and* the world's. Comfort zones stand between you and your full potential. Comfort zones prevent you from building your unapologetically authentic personal brand. Comfort zones hold you back from making a meaningful difference in the world.

The most inspirational people in the world are those who, quite simply, got uncomfortable. It's the people who reached an inflection point in their own lives and careers and took the leap to change. People who *became* the change. And what's more, it's the people who bravely, courageously, and often heroically shared it publicly.

Gabby Bernstein was a successful publicist in New York City, representing the hottest nightclubs in town. She was also an alcoholic and a cocaine addict. Fifteen years ago, she hit rock bottom, found Spirit, and got sober. Since that time, she has gone on to become one of the most spiritually influential people of our generation, preaching the power of miracles, manifestation, and mantras. Gabby has done "the work" not behind closed doors but rather boldly and publicly through her books, interviews, and on stages across the world.

Elizabeth Gilbert left her husband (the one she infamously fell in love with at the end of her bestselling book *Eat Pray Love*) to marry her best friend, who happened to be a woman. This decision did not lessen her fame, nor did it hinder the success of her book sales. Since that time, Gilbert has gone on to write two *New York Times* bestsellers (*Big Magic* and *City of Girls*), is regularly featured by TEDx and Oprah Winfrey discussing her marriage to Rayya Elias, and has grown her massively engaged online community to millions of loyal fans.

Political activist and NFL quarterback Colin Kaepernick refused to stand during the national anthem in protest of police brutality and racial inequality in the United States. This caused an uprising from the mass American public and even a denouncement from the president. In 2016, at the height of the controversy, he launched the Know Your Rights Campaign, an organization that held free seminars for disadvantaged youth to teach them about self-empowerment, American history, and legal rights.[1] In 2018, Nike released an ad featuring Kaepernick with the text, "Believe in something. Even if it means sacrificing everything."[2] Kaepernick was released by his contract with the San Francisco 49ers, and no team has picked him up since. He remains a free agent.

Are there people in the world who find Gabby Bernstein's message of meditation, miracles, and mantras too woo-woo? Most likely. Are there people in the world who disapprove of same-sex marriage and stopped following Elizabeth Gilbert? Without a doubt. And are there people in the world who vehemently disagreed with Colin Kaepernick's political statement during a national TV broadcast of America's most patriotic sports game? Clearly.

It's safe to say that it was *uncomfortable* for Gabby Bernstein, Elizabeth Gilbert, and Colin Kaepernick to share their truths with the world. It goes without saying that their truths made millions of other people uncomfortable too.

That's the whole fucking point.

Be loved or be hated but do not be ignored. This is how you make a true impact. This is how you change the world. This is what "living free" actually means. This is what it can actually do.

It's easy to spot when someone is stepping outside their comfort zone in the public arena when we look at well-known speakers, authors, and athletes like these. But heroic acts of "living free" and risking the potential of exposure, failure, rejection, and disapproval are actually happening all around us, all the time; with the people you know and love the most.

Naomi had been working for an insurance company as an internal wholesaler since she graduated from college. She loathed it. At age thirty-six, she gave birth to her first child and was so touched by her experience at the hospital working with her pediatric doctors, nurses, and sonographers, that she decided to quit her job and go back to school to get her degree in sonography. Everyone in her family was shocked. She and her husband fought for months as they struggled to find the money to cover costs for nannies and sitters and to support her going back to school. It took four years for Naomi to get her certification. Today, she works at a hospital, empowering her patients with all kinds of ailments to better understand their bodies. She wakes up every day, excited about life. She is a better wife and a better mom for it.

A single mom at forty-five years old, Alicia quit her high-powered, six-figure career working for the biggest agencies in the world to mentor female entrepreneurs. People thought she was crazy, as did she for quite some time. For a while, she bounced around consulting for a few start-ups, struggling to cover the bills, until she settled on one up-and-coming start-up agency. Within a year, the agency blossomed, as did Alicia's spirit. She lost twenty pounds, fell in love, and ended up taking a full-time role as chief operating officer.

After twenty years of being a trader, Brian knew he had to step away and start over. The industry had essentially imploded, and with no proper college degree and no other experience, he went through what can only be defined as an identity crisis. Over the course of a few years, he dug deep to understand who he was without his job title. He took on a new career in financial advising and eventually hired a life coach to support him through the transition. He now writes blogs on LinkedIn (many of which have gone viral) on how to create a life with meaning, rather than just make a living. His work is touching the lives of hundreds of people in his network and beyond.

Naomi is my sister-in-law, and I have never seen her so happy.

Alicia is my COO, and SimplyBe. is booming.

Brian is my husband, and he is thriving.

They are all my heroes. That's because they became their own first. Through a series of sleepless nights, tough decisions, outside judgments, and deep-seated fears, each of them had to step outside their own comfort zones in order to change their lives, and having done so, changed the lives of so many others.

Take stock of what keeps you comfortable. Whether it's your group of friends, your job, your romantic relationship, the place in which you live, what you eat, or even the stories you tell yourself in your mind. I guarantee there is at least one thing (if not a few) that resides inside your comfort zone that is not serving you.

It is in your willingness to get uncomfortable that you find your own heroism. It is in the decisions, choices, and experiences that scare you the most that you find your freedom, and thus your power. It is in the far-out edges beyond your comfort zone that your brand is born.

Be.

uncomfortable

Comfort zones keep you safe.
They also keep you small.

CHAPTER 22

FIND YOUR EDGES

"Can you remember who you were before
the world told you who you should be?"

Danielle LaPorte

Maybe you're not ready to quit your job, leave your marriage, come out of the closet, or start a political movement. That's fair. Finding freedom and living freely looks different to all of us.

I have found that the true power of freedom is found in the micro-actions of putting myself in scenarios that inspire me to simply see the world differently. That act alone is courageous. Whether it's listening to a podcast on a topic I disagree with, traveling to a place I have long been afraid to go, working with a coach who calls me out on my bullshit, or trying out a new physical activity that forces me to use my body in a new way—these are all *choices* I continually make that allow me to experience my power and my potential in a new light.

I call these my "edges." They are the outlets, people, places, and experiences that uplevel my life and have inspired me to live and lead with my own unapologetic authenticity. Busting out of my comfort zone has been the single most effective strategy for growth. What's more, it has not only given me my "content" to share an inspired message with my audience but it has also empowered me to relate to people on an entirely new level. My edges have dissolved my own judgments and fears, making room for real, genuine connection with other human beings. These connections are the foundation to everything there is to create: from a wildly successful career to a beautiful, meaningful life. Our connections to others make the world go 'round.

And it all begins with our connection to ourselves.

We can accelerate this connection within our edges. Here are the five most powerful edges I have pushed myself to feel into over the past ten years:

1. Travel
2. Masterminds, retreats, and workshops
3. Therapists, coaches, and healers
4. Disconnection
5. Breathwork, meditation, and movement

I describe each of these in more detail below, and because feeling into your own edges is a deeply personal act, I have also provided you with insights into how to take my edges and make them your own. It's time to leap.

THE TRAVEL EDGE

I'll never forget the moment I stepped foot in Thailand. I had gotten off the plane in Bangkok, checked into my hotel, and despite my wicked jet lag, hit the streets to take in the massive city. What struck me the most was not the wafting mouthwatering scents of street-food carts, the endless towering skyscrapers, or the deafening din of tuk tuks, motorcycles, and taxis, it was how insignificant I felt.

There I stood, on precisely the other side of the planet from where I live, as millions of passersby whirled around going about their days, considering nothing but their own lives. In that moment, I viscerally understood the enormity of the planet and had a game-changing epiphany: my problems, my dramas, my "stories" didn't matter.

Since then, I have sought to liberate myself from my own myopic worldview as much as I can. Over the past five years, I have learned that nothing opens my perspective, stimulates new ideas, and inspires gratitude more than travel. Whether it's accidentally tasting guinea pig in Ecuador, trekking through the Amazon riddled with insects the size of my hand, crying to God in a gothic church in Lisbon, sharing in a Shabbat dinner at a young couple's home in Jerusalem, learning how to properly exchange business cards in Singapore, staying in a home without running water in the Moroccan desert, or ascending to the fifth dimension with the help of a Balinese healer in his roadside shanty, one thing is for sure: I now see the world through a different lens. It's made me more compassionate, forgiving, accepting, brave, and to be frank, less high-maintenance. Above all, taking massive physical space away from work has empowered me to come back to it with revitalized energy and enthusiasm.

Make It Your Own: Perhaps jet-setting off to a foreign country isn't an option. You can still "travel" in your own life by exposing yourself to things you don't necessarily do on a regular basis. Throughout my travels, I have found it is not the places that open up my aperture, but the people I meet along the way. Instead of booking a plane ticket, book a dinner date with someone from another culture, religion, race, or country. Set the intention to ask questions and listen. You can create a connection with people in your own city who will inspire you to "travel" into new realms of thinking, seeing, and being.

THE MASTERMINDS, RETREATS, AND WORKSHOPS EDGE

What's better than investing in your own personal growth? Being surrounded by like-minded people investing in theirs. Events such as masterminds, conferences, retreats, and workshops are unparalleled "containers" for self-investigation, outward exploration, and collaborative learning. Sure, you can sit on a couch and talk about your problems to someone who is getting paid to listen to you. But it's an entirely different experience when you can sit around the breakfast table and go deep with people you just met. It sounds scary, but I have found that events such as these draw like-minded people, who are all on a similar spiritual wavelength or career path as I am, and safe space is inherently created in these environments. This leads to accelerated friendships, deep connections, and as a result, *real-time* transformation.

When I look back at some of the most defining moments of my life, especially in the past ten years as I have built my own brand, it was events like A-Fest, Summit, Mindvalley U, the Wright Foundation's Women's Essential Experience, Derek Halpern's Mastermind, and Baby Bathwater where I took leaps and bounds professionally, personally, and spiritually.

A "mastermind" can be a three-day experience, or a twelve-month program. The point of the experience is for participants to raise the bar by challenging each other and keeping each other accountable for creating and implementing their goals, all of which is usually facilitated by a coach. A "retreat" is generally true to its name, where you travel or retreat to a remote location to spend a concentrated amount of time (usually a few days to a few weeks at most) to dive deep on a particular theme, whether that be business, branding, wellness, purpose, yoga, or spirituality. Retreats are usually on the more intimate side, drawing as few as ten people or as many as one hundred. "Workshops" come in all shapes and sizes but commonly take place over the course of a few hours or up to a full day. They are intensive immersions, usually consisting of a mix of presentations, lectures, and experiential learning through breakouts, movement, and group sharing.

Make It Your Own: There are so many masterminds, retreats, and workshops on the market, it can be overwhelming when trying to decide where to start (not to mention expensive). I recommend starting your own mastermind by identifying a few people in your city, in your industry, or simply at a similar life stage as you. Set up a standing time to meet at least once a month, in person or via Zoom or Skype. You can build in a Facebook group, a WhatsApp group, or even a simple text chain to stay connected in between. The purpose of this group can be anything you want it to be: feedback, encouragement, accountability, inspiration. This is exactly what I did before I had the money or the courage to attend an actual event. If you're set on attending one, look to your favorite coaches, thought leaders, and experts to see if and when they might be hosting their next event. Mark the date and put a savings plan in place to make it a reality.

THE THERAPISTS, COACHES, AND HEALERS EDGE

I often say running a business is hard, but running a life is harder. As your business grows, so will you. You will inevitably need to hire a professional support staff to help your business thrive, but you will also need an emotional support staff to help *you* thrive. In full transparency, of all the things I have ever spent money on, from my home to my clothes to even the places I have traveled, nothing compares to the invaluable investments I have made in therapists, coaches, and healers.

In my twenties, I was grappling with a devastating heartbreak after the ending of a five-year relationship. I saw my therapist Abby literally once a week like clockwork for two years straight. Our work together helped me to heal my codependent romantic patterns and my low self-worth, which had been leading me to emotionally unavailable men my whole life.

Five years into running Cheeky, something felt terribly "off." I had started to suffer from constant anxiety attacks, chronic sinus infections, and toxic rage toward my business partner. So, I hired my life coach, Gina, who, through months of emotional breakdowns on her couch, gave me the simple permission to say out loud: "I don't think I want to do this anymore." This changed everything.

It was no surprise, however, that into my first few years running SimplyBe., I was operating out of pure reaction instead of a true strategy. I hired my business coach, Kirsten, who on our very first session told me I was completely leading with my ego. She was right. With her help, I established my company's core values and finally found my direction—and my integrity.

And just a few years ago, when SimplyBe. had become a seven-figure company within eighteen months, I crashed from physical burnout and knew that I had to heal my relationship to "hustle." So I hired Elena, my energy healer, who taught me how to actually, truly, honestly, and deeply *listen* to my body for the first time in my life.

My emotional support staff pushed me, expanded me, and allowed me to become the woman who is writing this book. Without them, I wouldn't be anywhere near as conscious, responsible, empathetic, and healthy as I am today. It's safe to say they saved my life. Life is hard . . . it's okay to accept that. We are not meant to do it alone.

Make It Your Own: I recognize it's a tall order to simply go out and hire an army of emotional support staff. And the truth is, it's not that simple. Finding the right coach, healer, or therapist is like finding the right romantic partner: you have to "click." It's a rare thing. To begin to feel into this edge, I recommend turning instead to the closest, most intuitive, and connected person in your life: you. Before I ever set foot in a therapist's office, I journaled. I have close to thirty journals that grace my home office shelves, dating back to the fifth grade. They saved my life as much as any person. Putting pen to paper and letting it flow can be extremely cathartic and as such, therapeutic. It's a wonderful starting point to gain clarity on what's working and feel into the edges of what's not. Commit to journaling every morning for twenty minutes straight. Try it out for a week and time yourself. Don't censor anything, just let it pour out. At the end of the week, reread your words. You will inevitably sense patterns you either wish to release or want to continue to grow.

THE DISCONNECTION EDGE

I took a trip to Bulgaria with my best friend, Megan, in the summer of 2019. We had been traveling for about a week, and neither one of us could relax. We couldn't put our finger on *why* until we ironically looked at *what* our fingers were quite literally on: our iPhones. We had traveled thousands of miles away from our day-to-day lives but there we were, consumed by the stress of work, distractions from friends and family, and our own addiction to social media. We were sitting at breakfast one morning in the beautiful mountains outside Melnik, poring over Instagram, when Megan looked up at me and exclaimed, "Jessica. Oh my god. We have got to get a fucking grip!" I couldn't have agreed with her more. We marched our way back to our hotel room, made a beeline for the safe, turned OFF our phones, and locked them up in our hotel room safe. We wrote out a pledge on a piece of hotel stationary that read, "Jessica Zweig and Megan Taylor hereby agree that they will not touch their phones for the next twenty-four hours." We signed it.

When I recall this story, I laugh out loud at the ridiculousness of it. But to be frank, it is the one and only day of our trip that I vividly remember. I can tell you the conversations we had, the details of the places we visited, and the emotions we both felt. When you turn off your devices (mainly your smartphones and computers), it allows you to become radically present, provides deep focus, and restores brainwaves and neuroplasticity, which is essential for ideation, creativity, memory, and connection. It's impossible to show up as your fully expressed, authentic self if you are sitting around scrolling all day. Show up for your communities, companies, and clients by shutting it down and showing up for yourself first. Turn off your phone. Turn on your power.

Make It Your Own: Disconnecting from technology is uncomfortable as hell. The truth is, our dependency on our phones is real. Many of us feel we NEED to be connected 24/7, and most of us actually are. But even carving out a small patch of time to disconnect can return your energy to its natural state, clear your mind, and invigorate your spirit. I suggest choosing microsprints of time, where you completely disconnect for an hour, then a few, then an entire day, and maybe even days at a time. The best way to keep yourself accountable to this is to call upon your accountability buddy! I would never have stuck to the committed plan of twenty-four hours without my phone in Bulgaria had it not been for Megan, who was right there with me doing it too. Make this a regular practice, and watch how you become increasingly comfortable in the simple art of doing nothing and the beautiful act of simply being.

THE BREATHWORK, MEDITATION, AND MOVEMENT EDGE

Years ago, before I had ever built a business, crossed an ocean, started up an Instagram account, or even considered the idea of a "personal brand," I would ride my bike for hours along Lake Michigan in downtown Chicago practically every day. I had just moved to the city to become an actress and was waitressing at night, providing me what felt like endless time each day to, well . . . *be* with myself. I didn't realize at the time just how precious that was. Looking back, I now see how my bike rides *were* my meditations. I felt so connected to my body, my mind, and most of all, my heart during those rides. As I have gotten older, my time has become more limited, while the emphasis on the importance of meditation has only increased. I often feel legit pressure to sit cross-legged, close my eyes, breathe in through my nose and out through my mouth and, you know, clear my head. Sometimes I do that, or at least try. But to be frank, I find many traditional meditation practices limiting, confining, and honestly, downright hard to do. The times when I feel the most connected to my body, which leads me to connect to my breath, which leads me to become deeply present and therefore in my heart and ultimately in my joy is when I simply do what makes me feel good. *This* is my form of meditation.

Sometimes it's still a bike ride. Other times, it's a deep, juicy yoga class. Often, it's me sitting on a meditation pillow mentally chanting a mantra. Every now and then, it's a powerful breathwork meditation, guided by a shaman. But most of the time, my meditation is an everyday act like cooking my husband a delicious dinner. Or losing myself in a novel. It's also losing myself in the warm fur of my dogs as I snuggle with them for hours. And once in a while, it's losing myself on the dance floor at a sweaty nightclub filled with house music alongside my girlfriends. I have found that the more I try to label meditation as "right" or "wrong," the more confining it is. Fuck the rules. Breathe in silence or scream at the top of your lungs. Stay still for an hour or gyrate until 3:00 a.m. It doesn't matter. Change your vibration, change your life, and find your own edge.

Do what makes you feel good. This alone is a revolutionary act.

Make It Your Own: Ask yourself the following questions: "What actually decreases my stress?" "What gets me out of my head and into my heart?" "How can I increase my ability to connect to my intuition?" "What does it take for me to show up as my highest self?" Write out your answers to these questions. There are a million possibilities here. For some, this might look like getting up at 5:00 a.m. to meditate. For others, this looks like clocking an extra hour of sleep. Whatever it is, let it be YOUR version of meditation. And then, practice, practice, practice. Your edges are always available to you.

Be.

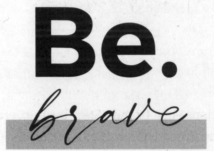

When you meet your fear, you find
your power. When you push past your
edges, you become unlimited.
The sky is the beginning.

SIMPLY BE.

"Legacy is greater than currency."

Gary Vaynerchuk

Congratulations, my friend. Step-by-step, you've built your own guide and unearthed your authentic truth.

You possess the knowingness to share it in the service of others and a road map to do so. You are fully equipped to stand in your power offline as much as on, armed with tactics to leave a meaningful impression and strategies to live an ever-evolving existence filled with edges. You are ready to make your message your mission. You are ready to transform your mission into your masterpiece.

None of it is bullshit.

But the work of building your personal brand doesn't stop here. This is just the beginning. As you fully embody your authentic self, both online and off, and walk through the world (whether that be within the four walls of your office, on your Instagram profile, or simply down the street), remember that you are inspiring people by proxy with your sheer freedom of simply being. As a result, you will create a halo effect of courage. You will become the example of what it looks like to live your truth. You will inadvertently give people permission to be themselves too. And in turn, you will set everyone around you free. You will set the world free. And what a world it would be if we all woke up to our own authentic power and used our voices, our platforms, and our brands to inspire others to simply be. An infinite awakening would occur. It starts with you—right here, right now.

I explained earlier that the biggest secret about personal branding is that no one cares about you. That's actually the second biggest secret. The biggest secret of them all when it comes to building a personal brand is this:

You are your own fucking superpower. Just you. As you are. Simply being.

You were born, and therefore you are important.

You breathe, and therefore you matter.

You exist, and therefore you are worthy of having, achieving, and experiencing everything and anything you could ever want.

This simple act of believing in your self-worth, sharing your brand, and simply being you is the key to building your notoriety, growing your impact, and increasing your net worth. It's the key to building a personal brand that will change lives, while you live a life beyond your wildest dreams. You deserve it all, my friend.

Simply being isn't just your greatest opportunity, it's your greatest responsibility. Not just to yourself and the people you serve but to the world.

Don't let us down.

Simply Be.

And set the world free.

AFTERWORD

As I made the drive back to the city in my beat-up Honda with a $500 check in hand signed by my father, I got a download. Despite the humiliation and within the weeping, I felt a sensation of clarity: "I am abundant."

I just kept saying this over and over again in my mind:

I am abundant because . . . I have a roof over my head.

I am abundant because . . . I have gas in my car right now.

I am abundant because . . . my brother called me this morning to say hi.

I am abundant because . . . I enjoy writing with blue pens and I own dozens of them.

I am abundant because . . . my dog Zooey will be wagging her tail when I get home.

I am abundant because . . . I have working heat.

I am abundant because . . . I am breathing.

I started to feel it in my body. I began to vibrate with a sense of peace, of love, of clarity. Peace that I was, and always will be, okay. Love for every little last thing in my life. Clarity that I, Jessica, inherently have value despite what's in my bank account. I clung to this vibration of knowingness and let it form an imprint within my being. I could not and would not ever lose this feeling.

That day, I made a pact with myself that I was going to stop play- ing the victim and take full responsibility for my one precious life. I was also going to start honoring all that I *did* have and look at my life through the lens of gratitude. I decided that I was indeed rich with blessings. That fateful Sunday morning asking my parents to help me pay my phone bill at thirty-three years old was the end of the road of worthlessness.

There was no going back.

Not too shortly thereafter, I got a call from a dear colleague who had just gotten a consulting contract and needed some extra help. She asked me to partner up with her on the account and offered me $5,000 a month in retainer. It was more money than I had ever made, and I was shell-shocked. I remember her saying, "I believe in paying good people good money."

It was a clear moment of validation. Yet, had I not already made the shift to choosing that I was worthy of it, it would have only been a temporary high. I don't know if I would have been able to fully receive her offer. I don't mean in my bank account; I mean in my soul.

That's when everything shifted. Right there. That was the moment I knew the imprint was there to stay. That was the moment my life, my business, and my brand began to metamorphose.

Over the past decade, as my net worth has grown, I have learned that my personal brand has been the ultimate vehicle to my success. It's been how I have attracted unparalleled opportunity and unlimited growth.

But my self-worth has been and always will be the catalyst. It's a knowingness I cannot and will not ever unlearn. I now know that I will only be able to command the money I believe I am worthy of making. I now know that I will only be able to experience true abundance when I cherish what I already have. I now know that I will only be able to authentically put my brand out into the world if I am willing to honestly share my failures alongside my successes. I now know that I will only be able to free myself from my insecurities, my undeservingness, and my imposter syndrome when I give myself the permission to *be*.

This is my daily practice, my holiest prayer, my most sacred commitment. Life is precious. And I am my own most precious asset.

I will never stop investing in me.

ACKNOWLEDGMENTS

This is a book about learning how to become the person you are meant to be. I can wholeheartedly say that I would not be who I am, or where I am, without the following people. It really does take a village to run a business, write a book, live a life, chase your dreams, and fully believe in your own light.

To my father, Ron: thank you for showing me the real-life example of what it means to be a true, self-made entrepreneur. You have single-handedly taught me the power of tenacity, integrity, and service. I would not be the woman, nor the businesswoman, I am today without your wisdom, selflessness, and unconditional love.

To my mother, Suzanne, my earth angel: thank you for being my role model of kindness, compassion, empathy, and nonjudgment. You are my treasure trove of truth and my very best friend. Baba is smiling down on both of us, shining her blessings and pride on us forever and always.

To one of the most exceptional human beings I know, let alone share blood with, my one and only brother, Doug: thank you for rooting for me like no one else ever has. I am able to stand taller because of it. I would have chosen you as a best friend if I hadn't been lucky enough to get you as a brother. To my sister-in-law, Naomi: thank you for being the sister I never had but always wanted and then some. To my perfect little nephews Isaiah and Emmanuel: may you grow up to simply be all you want to be too.

To my soul sister from another mister Megan Taylor: thank you for opening my eyes to the profound power of adventure. Our friendship is a work of art, and it has made me a better human being. I could not live without you in my life, by my side, every moment of the day. Thirteen countries, thousands of belly laughs, a million memories, and counting. Let's keep going forever.

To my number 2, my ninja, my unicorn, my starseed sister Aleksa Narbutaitis. This book wouldn't have come to fruition without SimplyBe., and SimplyBe. would never have been anything without you. Thank you for your gorgeous designs for this book, your inspired leadership, and above all, your friendship. I am infinitely grateful that you walked into my life when you did. We are living proof that the Universe always has bigger, better, and brighter plans for us. Here's to JZAN, forever and into the next lifetime. I'm positive we'll meet each other there.

To my curious one Nora Shepard: watching you grow into all you have become is like witnessing a masterpiece of female empowerment. Knowing that I played one tiny part in it will be my legacy. Thank you for taking SimplyBe. to the sky with me. It's always just the beginning.

To the SimplyBe. team Julia Addis, Shaun Kimbrow, Kristin Rohlwing, Shervin Bain, Bryan Carter, Arianne Payne, Gary Stallings and our ever-growing roster of rock stars: thank you for driving the dream. Your talent, passion, dedication, and most of all, your character, honesty, and integrity is the fabric of SimplyBe. You are the example of simply being—bringing your own humanity and authenticity to your work and changing lives every damn day, including mine. Leading you is my life's greatest honor.

To my soul sister, biggest inspiration, and ultimate cheerleader Rea Frey. This book came to be because you pushed me to do it in the first place. Thank you for relentlessly believing in me more than I believed in myself. It has been the secret sauce to my success.

To my girl gang—Sara Shankman, Betsey Nooney, Megan Hirschey, Kendra Peterson, Nadia Wetzel, Tiffany Louise, Brita Collier, Katy Wilson, and Laura Holloway: thank you for teaching me the life-changing, sacred magic of true girlfriends.

To my truest bluest Hedy Dietzen: thank you for your undying sisterhood, loyalty, and love. No matter where life leads us, you will always be my home.

To the sunshine of my life James Goeke: thank you for filling the void in my heart I didn't even know I had with your love, laughter, and light. As long as I have you, James, I know my life will be Light.

To my life-support hotline Polly Jo Monson: green glitter eye shadow for life and don't you ever let me forget it. I know you won't. Thank you for letting me awkwardly touch your face all those years ago. I don't know where I would have ended up if I hadn't.

To my soul sister Tali Kogan: our friendship can only be defined as predestined. You have given me more confidence in my own light than I can describe in words. Thank you for your genius vision on this book. Having you in my life has empowered me to shine brighter and believe in my beauty, from the inside out. I am forever grateful I found you.

To Alida Miranda-Wolff: you are sacred stitching to the fabric of SimplyBe. Thank you for always rooting for me, for opening doors for me, and for holding space for my metamorphosis as a leader with so much empathy and love.

To my mentor Denise Senter: thank you for giving me every single opportunity to know my own potential. I am the executive I am today because of you.

To my extended family of The SimplyBe. Agency. In no particular order: Gertrude and Rich Lyons, Larry Jordan, Andrew Walker, Avanti Kumar Singh, Florence Ann Romano, Payal Beri, Shelley Paxton, Andrea Levoff, Nicholas Moriarity, Dana Frost, Jason Hospodka, Aine Rock, Leslie Waltke, Linda Neff, Tracy Ftacek, Lola Wright, Stephen Taylor, Subhi Barakat, Erin Coupe, Erik Severinghaus, Robbin Carroll, Alexa Martinez, Irene Wood, Carestha Widjaja, Jason Rosenthal, Kyle Schauenberg, Earnest Sweat, Jacopo Bracco, Tony Wilkins, Ladi Greenstreet, Ruggero Gramatica, and Patrick Cullen. Helping you to build your brands is my life's work. Thank you for trusting me, trusting yourself, and in turn, helping to power SimplyBe. into the organization it is today. It is never lost on me.

To my X-men coach and one of my biggest inspirations, Nicole Arbour: thank you for seeing in me what I couldn't see in myself but always knew was there. You light up the world with your authenticity and as such have trailblazed the way for so many of us. #GOTEAM.

To Dana Nicole Anderson: thank you for your wisdom and your support of me and this book. Most of all, thank you for your willingness to shine a life-changing mirror my way. I will forever be grateful that our souls collided.

To my phenomenal agent, Marilyn Allen: thank you for being a light on this path and making this experience nothing short of magical. To Sarah Hall and Bonnie Rice: thank you for seeing me and believing in me. To my incredible editor, Diana Ventimiglia, my fantastic audio producer, Jeff Mack, and my entire Sounds True family: thank you for believing in this message and for quite literally making my dreams come true. And thank you to Lori Harder for the assist.

To my coaches, gurus, and teachers—Gina Marotta, Tony Hunter, Kirsten Zoub, Elena Bensonoff, and Abby Miller: thank you for never letting me settle for anything else besides my own truth.

To my virtual community and every single person I have interacted with along this journey: whether you have sent an email, attended a workshop, left a comment on an Instagram post, come up to me after a talk, or read this book, I see you, I love you, and I am so deeply grateful for you. Your commitment to simply being all YOU want to be inspires me more than you could ever possibly know. Everything I do, I do for you.

To my angels, ancestors, spirit guides, higher masters, loved ones, Pleia-dians, and the infinite Universe: thank you for the protection, information, and abundant blessings you have given to me while being here during this tiny microcosm of time I have as Jessica. I promise to not let you down.

And finally, to my husband, Brian Fisher: no one has ever let me simply be me the way you have. Your love set me free. And although your love and support have allowed me to expand into new worlds, both figuratively and literally, nothing will ever compare to the completion I experience when I am next to you. Whether we're traveling the world, or snuggling with Don and Zooey, one thing is always clear: I freaking love doing life with you. Thank you for being my rock, my knight, my champion, my endless laughter, my mirror, my teacher, my partner, my best friend, and the wind beneath my wings. You are the greatest per-son I have ever known. I am, because of you.

NOTES

Chapter 1. Embrace Your Shit

1. Taylor Dunn, "Gary Vaynerchuk on How to Quit Your Day Job," ABC News, March 31, 2018, accessed January 2020, abcnews.go.com/Business/gary-vaynerchuk-quit-day-job/story?id=54130708.

2. Jeff Fromm, "How Unilever Is Winning with Millennials and Gen Z," *Forbes*, accessed January 2020, forbes.com/sites/jefffromm/2017/01/31/how-unilever-is-winning-with-millennials-and-gen-z-/#466a67d352fd.

Chapter 2. No One Cares

1. "Leveraging the Value of Emotional Connection for Retailers," Motista, accessed January 2020, motista.com/resource/leveraging-value-emotional-connection-retailers.

Chapter 5. How to Play the (Long) Game

1. Bryan Robinson, "Are You Suffering from Burnout? Here Are Signs of the Invisible Disease," *Forbes*, accessed January 2020, forbes.com/sites/bryanrobinson/2019/06/02/the-burnout-club-now-considered-a-disease-with-a-membership-price-you-dont-want-to-pay-for-success/#8e2c9e37ab0d.

2. Elizabeth Hampson and Ushma Soneji, "At a Tipping Point? Workplace Mental Health and Well-Being," Deloitte, March 2017, accessed January 2020, www2.deloitte.com/content/dam/Deloitte/uk/Documents/public-sector/deloitte-uk-workplace-mental-health-n-wellbeing.pdf.

Chapter 6. Your Mess(age) Is Your Magic

1. J. Clement, "Number of Facebook Users Worldwide 2015–2020," Statista, November 15, 2019, accessed January 2020, statista.com/statistics/490424/number-of-worldwide-facebook-users.

2. Kit Smith, "52 Fascinating and Incredible YouTube Statistics," Brandwatch, July 15, 2019, accessed January 2020, brandwatch.com/blog/youtube-stats/.

3. "46 Eye Opening LinkedIn Statistics for 2020," 99firms, May 9, 2019, accessed January 2020, 99firms.com/blog/linkedin-statistics/#gref.

4. "Twitter by the Numbers: Stats, Demographics and Fun Facts, Omnicore, September 5, 2019, accessed January 2020, omnicoreagency.com/twitter-statistics/.

5. Maryam Moshin, "10 Instagram Stats Every Marketer Should Know in 2020," November 29, 2019, accessed January 2020, Oberlo, oberlo.com/blog/instagram-stats-every-marketer-should-know.

6. J. Clement, "Global Digital Population as of October 2019," Statista, November 20, 2019, accessed January 2020, statista.com/statistics/617136/digital-population-worldwide/.

Chapter 7. Introducing the Personal Brand Hologram

1. Oprah Winfrey Leadership Academy for Girls, accessed January 2020, owlag.co.za.

Chapter 8. Create Endless Content with the Supernova

1. Arianna Huffington, "10 Years Ago, I Collapsed from Burnout and Exhaustion, and It's the Best Thing That Could Have Happened to Me," Medium, April 6, 2017, medium.com/thrive-global/10-years-ago-i -collapsed-from-burnout-and-exhaustion-and-its-the-best-thing -that-could-have-b1409f16585d.

Chapter 14. Pitch Like a Pro

1. Hana Muasher, "New Muck Rack Survey: 3% of Journalists Say They Rely Heavily on Press Releases Sent Via Newswires," March 22, 2018, accessed January 2020, Muck Rack, muckrack.com/blog/.

2. Haje Jan Kamps, "Who Are Twitter's Verified Users?" Medium, May 25 2015, medium.com/@Haje/who-are-twitter-s-verified-users-af976fc1b032.

Chapter 15. Get Your (Social Media) Mind Right

1. Mary Kekatos, "Teens Who Spend More Than Three Hours a Day on Social Media Are at Higher Risk for Mental Health Issues, Study Finds," Daily-Mail.com, September 11, 2019, accessed January 2020, dailymail.co.uk/ health/article-7452477/.

2. SWNS, "Americans Check Their Phones 80 Times a Day: Study," NewYork-Post, November 7, 2018, accessed January 2020, nypost.com/2017/11/08 /americans-check-their-phones-80-times-a-day-study/.

Chapter 18. Color Your Life

1. Jena McGregor, "The Art of Mark Zuckerberg's Hoodie," Washington Post, May 10, 2012, accessed January 2020, washingtonpost.com/blogs/ post-leadership/post/the-art-of-mark-zuckerbergs-hoodie/2012/05/09 /gIQAhBCnDU_blog.html.

2. Noelle Mateer, "Remember When Hillary Clinton Wore a Pantsuit in Her First Lady Portrait?" CNN, August 2, 2019, accessed January 2020, cnn. com/style/article/hillary-clinton-pantsuit-remember-when/index.html.

3. Olivia Le Poidevin and Trystan Young, "Why Did Millions Join Secret Face-book Group Pantsuit Nation?" BBC, November 15, 2016, accessed January 2020, bbc.com/news/av/election-us-2016-37987616/.

4. Le Poidevin and Young, "Why Did Millions Join."

Chapter 21. Be Your Own Hero

1. Know Your Rights Campaign, accessed January 2020, knowyourrightscamp.com/.

2. "Nike Releases Full Ad Featuring Colin Kaepernick-Video," *Guardian*, September 7, 2018, accessed January 2020, theguardian.com/sport/ video/2018/sep/07/nike-releases-full-ad-featuring-colin-kaepernick-video.

ABOUT THE AUTHOR

Jessica Zweig is the CEO of the SimplyBe. Agency, a premier personal branding firm based in Chicago, serving clients across the globe. Jessica was named by Crain's Business as one of 2020's Most Notable Entrepreneurs, as the 2018 and 2019 Stevie® Award winner for Female Entrepreneur of the Year, a Top Digital Marketer to Watch by *Inc.*, and a Personal Branding Expert by *Forbes*.

The SimplyBe. Agency helps its clients, ranging from corporate executives to entrepreneurs and creatives, in becoming recognized industry experts and thought leaders. Jessica frequently facilitates sold-out workshops and global masterminds and speaks on the power of personal branding to corporations such as Google, Pinterest, Salesforce, Morningstar, Mars, Blackstone, EQ Office, Motorola, Beam Suntory, Nike, Red Bull, the *Chicago Tribune*, Virgin, and Bank of America.

Her work has been featured in MarketWatch, Business Insider, Thrive Global, the Newsette, and Create + Cultivate, among others. She is a regular correspondent on Chicago's FOX, ABC, NBC, and WCIU networks as a personal branding and social media expert.

She is host of the top-ranked marketing podcast, The SimplyBe. Podcast, where she interviews today's top entrepreneurs, CEOs, influencers, thought leaders, and authors on how to build your brand and live your best, most authentic life.

On a mission to debunk the perception that personal branding is an act of vanity, Jessica believes that, when done right, personal branding is an act of service, a social responsibility, and a positive investment toward a positive future.

Jessica lives in Chicago with her husband and her two dogs, Zooey and Don Julio.

ABOUT SOUNDS TRUE

Sounds True is a multimedia publisher whose mission is to inspire and support personal transformation and spiritual awakening. Founded in 1985 and located in Boulder, Colorado, we work with many of the leading spiritual teachers, thinkers, healers, and visionary artists of our time. We strive with every title to preserve the essential "living wisdom" of the author or artist. It is our goal to create products that not only provide information to a reader or listener but also embody the quality of a wisdom transmission.

For those seeking genuine transformation, Sounds True is your trusted partner. At SoundsTrue.com you will find a wealth of free resources to support your journey, including exclusive weekly audio interviews, free downloads, interactive learning tools, and other special savings on all our titles.

To learn more, please visit SoundsTrue.com/freegifts or call us toll-free at 800.333.9185.

sounds true
WAKING UP THE WORLD